Bond Halbert Publishing
7510 Sunset Blvd. #1020
Los Angeles, CA 90046
www.bondhalbert.com
310-367-5321

Foreword

Even if you are not in marketing or interested in making a lot of money really really fast, what you are about to read will change your life forever.

It may sound too fantastic to believe, but it is true.

You see, the letters which make up this book were written by Gary C. Halbert whose hard-hitting, no-B.S. Style, coupled with a brilliant and experienced marketing mind, is nothing short of a mental kick to the head which will give you a real inside look at <u>exactly</u> how to create great marketing campaigns that make millions upon millions of dollars.

Many people consider Gary Halbert to be the greatest copywriter in history, and they make a great case.

Gary has had more multi-million dollar winning campaigns in more industries than any other copywriter, living or dead.

His sales letters, ads, and other promotions have generated sales which can only be measured in the BILLIONS.

But, Gary Halbert was far more than the Top Gun of copywriters, and he was far more than a marketing maverick. He was also a great mentor to many of today's best copywriters and to his many fans from around the world, who read his breakthrough newsletter, The Gary Halbert Letter.

To them and many more of today's top money makers, he was simply a godsend.

Besides being the guy who wrote one of the most widely mailed sales letter in history, Gary had a really eccentric and fascinating life.

His tale is a true rags to riches story and he once wrote…"I have been robbed, tied up, gagged, blindfolded, threatened. I've made and lost millions. I have been eulogized, ostracized, and plagiarized. I've also… been both a prison guard and a prison inmate."

It was during his ten months in California's Boron Federal Prison Camp the letters in this book were written to his youngest son, me.

The Boron Letters are, without doubt, his most personal work. And since they were published, the no-holds-barred letters have become a cult classic among marketers for good reason.

The simple letters were designed to be a crash course on direct marketing, as well as a crash course on life. The letters were never meant to be republished as-is. However, they were eventually published as-is, and the lessons in them have since changed many lives.

To this day, I receive phone calls, letters, and communications from around the world from grateful fans testifying how the Boron Letters have changed their lives.

These letters are the greatest gift I have ever received, and in a short while you will see exactly why.

As I said, these money making lessons were written in prison. When you are surrounded by every imaginable kind of felon from coke dealers, mafia hit men, common murderers, motorcycle maniacs, bank robbers, embezzlers etc. you don't, as my pop says, "pussy foot around."

Prison conversations are blunt and to the point. So are these letters.

The letters are a stripped down version of the most important secrets Gary ever learned about how to make a fortune, and they explain exactly how to develop a "killer" marketing appeal from the ground up.

The wisdom in the book covers everything from layout to offer development and list selection; how to create a winning game plan… and… everything in this book will also help you create a profitable website.

Here, I will let my pop tell you all about what's in these letters in his own words.

- **The *basics* of writing good copy!**

- The <u>fine points</u> of writing good copy!

- **What *really* makes people buy!**

- How to lead your reader by the hand!

- **Why you never get a second chance to make a first impression… and… why you must "hook" your reader from the moment he *sees* your copy!**

- How to give ads and letters the right "look"!

- **Secrets of order pulling layouts!**

- An essay on closing the sale!

- ***Exactly* how to ask for an order!**

- What you can learn from Alex Haley and his book, <u>Roots</u>!

- **How to make your copy clear and readable!**

- The <u>surest</u> way to become a big money writer!

- **Why you should write for money… and *not*… for applause!**

- What to do when you don't know what to do!

- **How to turn a losing catalog into a multi-million dollar success!**

- Halt: How memorizing that acronym can keep you out of a <u>lot</u> of trouble!

- **A prison inmate's "street smart" survival kit!**

- Why "make a bushel of money" works better than "increase your income"!

- **Six secrets of special deals you can write about in your letters!**

- A little trick every copywriter should know!

- **7 exact steps to direct mail success!**

- The most common marketing mistakes made by beginners!

- **How to keep going when the going is hard!**

- How to <u>imprint</u> the process of writing good ad copy on your nerves, muscle fibers, brain cells and every part of your physical and mental being!

- **An emotional "tool kit" which can save your life!**

- The most important key to making <u>really</u> <u>serious</u> money!

- **How to become a student of markets!**

- How to use the *SRDS* list book to make a fortune!

- **A discussion of a 156-million dollar promotion!**

- Cheap research: How to <u>make</u> <u>sure</u> you'll hit the right nerve!

- **Examples of winning formulas and "double customization"!**

- How to get flowing again when you're stuck!

- **How to discover the right central selling idea!**

- How to use envelopes to induce guilt!

- **A good "boilerplate" P.S. that can make you money!**

- How to get orders from people who have already decided <u>not</u> to order!

- **The best attention grabbers in the world!**

- How to make your reader "picture with pleasure" what you are trying to sell!

- **The *ultimate* layout for an order coupon!**

- 8 things you should have at hand <u>before</u> you start to write an ad or direct mail piece!

- **What you must *always* include in your marketing research!**

- How to manufacture the "aha" experience!

Of course you are not going to learn just about making money. This book has personal advice and interesting stories as well.

So sit back, read, learn, laugh and enjoy your new and improved outlook on life.

Sincerely,
Bond Halbert

P.S.: Like many others, you might find yourself addicted to Gary's writing. If you do crave more effective money making tips, we got your fix at TheGaryHalbertLetter.com The letters on the website are 100% free.

The Boron Letters
Chapter 1

Tuesday, 5:41 p.m.
June 12, 1984

Dear Bond,

   This letter is going to be the first in a long series of letters in which I will attempt to communicate to you a lot of the important things I have learned in the last 46 years.

   I am going to try to teach you what I have learned about selling by mail, getting and staying healthy, how to get along with people, and, in general, how to have a good life without getting yourself all screwed up. There will also be stuff about sex, drugs, and rock and roll! I'm going to try to write to you every day of the week (except Sunday) and spend about one hour on each letter. That way, by the time I get out of here, we should have covered a lot of ground.

   Also, I intend to reread these letters myself after I am finished and use them as source material for a book I have wanted to write for a long time. The book, unless I come up with a better title, will be called:

How To Be Your Own Messiah

   These letters will ramble around somewhat. I'm going to try to keep the flow going so I am not going to slow down to edit these letters and, therefore, don't expect them to be as precisely written as my ads and other writings.

   Anyway, let's get started. As you know, today is my birthday and, strange as it may seem, it hasn't been a bad one under the circumstances. For one thing, I got your birthday letter and the cards your Mom sent me and, for another, today is the first day I was able to run "the hill" non-stop. Being able to do that really made me feel good. The hill is a real son of a gun. It is very steep and, by my calculations, it is about 8/10 of a mile. I went around the hill 5 times for a total of 4 miles and, as I said, on one of those circuits (the third one), I did it running (actually it was more of a slow jog) non-stop.

   You know what? When I came in here, just three weeks ago, it was hard for me just to <u>walk once</u> around that darn hill. And, before I am finished, I'll bet you I can run around that hill ten times (8 miles) without stopping.

Well, anyway, this all leads me to the first and most important thing I want to write about, which is improving and maintaining your health and physical fitness. I'll have a lot more to say about this subject later, but today, I just want to "warm up" a little bit and tell you a few good ideas that you can start using every day. The first thing I want to talk about is "road work." Road work is walking, jogging and running. And, in my opinion, you should do about one hour of road work every day of the week except Sunday. I believe the best time to do your road work is right after you get out of bed.

In fact, in my opinion, the best groove to get into is get out of bed, (early) wash your face, brush your teeth, use the bathroom, etc., and then, eat a piece of fruit (I think a banana is the best) and then hit the street! That's it. Just get out that front door and start moving. Walk, run, jog. Keep moving for about 1/2 hour and then turn around and come back. You know, I really do believe this is the very best way in the world to start the day. It cleans you out, it settles you down and it gives you a nice glow that will stay with you throughout the day. It will also make you more clearheaded and improve the quality of your thinking. The benefits are enormous and, believe me, if you start doing this right away (like the day after you get this letter!) it won't be long at all untill you become positively addicted to your early morning workout.

By the way, this addiction is not just psychological. It is a real honest-to-God drug addiction. But don't let that scare you. This is what's known as a positive addiction. A positive addiction is simply being addicted to something (like exercise) that improves the quality of your life. A negative addiction, on the other hand, is being addicted to something (like cigarettes) that lowers the quality of your life.

What happens when you do road work is that, after about forty minutes, your brain begins to secrete what some people refer to as "survival chemicals." The names of these chemicals, as far as I know, are beta endorphins and norepinephrine. Some people say these chemicals are 200 times stronger than morphine and, in my opinion, the feeling you get is sort of like a good drug high, except that the "high" is not artificial, and you become zestful rather than speedy and, unlike a drug high, this is a high that is good for you.

If I seem to be going on and on about this, it is because it is so important, and it is something you can do right away! And, actually, of everything I have learned about in my entire life, this stuff about doing road work the first thing in the morning is very close to being the most important thing of all.

So I really hope you get started on this morning road work program as soon as you get this letter, and I also hope it becomes a habit for all the rest of your life.

I Love You and Good Luck!
Dad

P.S. Please get me a copy of "The Joy of Running" by Theodore Kostrubala.

6:43 PM

UPDATE:

This first letter is actually designed to remind me of many lessons my father had taught me before leaving for Boron so allow me to bring the reader up to speed.

The lesson on health is crystal clear, and there is a reason it comes FIRST.

Dad's father died at the young age of 59 from heart failure, and that spooked him, just as my father's early death has spooked me.

For the first half of my pop's life he abused his body with junk food and a whole lot of booze.

Although he ate bad food, he really loved vegetables, even as a kid.

My grandma told me he never left the house without a book and a pocket full of veggies.

Later he would become a health nut and then settle into a pattern of falling in and out of exercising.

So yes, he was on a health kick while writing this letter and entering what he would always maintain was the healthiest period of his entire life, but…

The reason this is at the top of a series of letters about business is he knew

How You Feel Affects How You Think

This is why writers need a strict routine which gives them the best possible chance to be in a pretty good mood for work.

Even during his heavy drinking days, Gary Halbert would take his car in, eat right, and nourish his brain with books and movies to get back to work.

Another little side note is my father felt people worked better hungry which is why he didn't go for big breakfasts.

Anyway, there is another lesson he didn't outright express in this first part of the letter.

When he talks about how when he first got to Boron, he had a hard time just walking around the hill, and very soon he was running up it.

The lesson isn't just keep at it.

Right after I got my first mountain bike, I decided to ride it from Sunset Blvd. to Mulholland Dr. by way of a three-mile road that varied from around 3 degrees to what felt like 45 degrees in some spots.

The first day I went to conquer the hill, I made it a whopping 1/8th of a mile before collapsing in defeat. I decided to try again the next day, only this time…. I vowed to get off and walk if I had to.

Knowing this was going to be tough, I decided to try and peddle in a gear that seemed too easy.

Well, I am sure you can guess the end of this story. Yes I made it all the way up on my second attempt and the moral isn't just to not give up.

The moral of my dad's workout story and mine is the same and it applies to all of life…

Try Things At Least Twice

Just the second attempt at anything hard will be much easier. Not a little bit but by A LOT. It is true of almost everything, not just sports.

All first attempts are sloppy and lame. Most people will quit after their first experience with things that don't go so well, but if you are like my pop and me, then you KNOW that the first attempt is almost destined to fail.

You will learn enough to get a better assessment of the whole picture and what it will really takes to attain a goal on your second attempt.

Just that much more effort will propel you ahead of 95% of everyone walking the earth.

The sad part is, we all already know this lesson, but we have to remind ourselves of it. Anyone who ever learned to ride a bike remembers their first attempt to learn because it ended with blood. Oops, anyone old enough not to have the advantage of today's protective gear that is.

As people get older, they start to decide whether they like stuff based on their first experience. Maybe you can't teach an old dog new tricks simply because, if he doesn't get it the first time he gives up.

Everyone wants to climb the mountain, but the big difference between those at the top and those still on the bottom is simply a matter of showing up tomorrow to give it just one more shot.

The Boron Letters
Chapter 2

Wednesday, 6:57 p.m.
June 13, 1984

Dear Bond,

   Today I crossed some sort of invisible mental line. It happened when I went for my initial meeting with the people who run the camp here and found out that they are total jerks. What happened as a result of that is that instead of being down and depressed, I just got tougher. Perhaps I'll write more about my new "get tough" attitude in a later letter, but for now, I want to get right back to this road work business.

   You know Bond, I can't stress how strongly I feel that doing an hour's worth of road work is perhaps the number one most valuable habit you can cultivate. You see, if you start your day this way, it will get you off to a great start. It will vastly improve the rest of your day since it will drain off a lot of tension and anxiety and, in general, it will clear out your mind so you can think better all day long!

   Plus, after you get into it, it will make you feel great!

   So anyway, here are some other good health habits that I think you should get into right away.

   FASTING - You are, in my opinion, too young to go on any extended fasts but I really think it would be good for you to fast one (1) full day each week.

   Currently, I am fasting every Saturday. And, I intend to keep fasting one day a week (at least) for the rest of my life. When you fast, you begin to normalize your body functions and also, you develop a certain self-discipline that will help you in most other areas of your life. I intend to write a lot more about fasting later on, but for right now, I just want to encourage you to begin immediately to fast one day every week.

   Here are some tips. First of all, I suggest you do not tell other people what you are doing. Most people don't understand fasting and all you will get from them on this subject is a lot of ignorant babble. Secondly, I feel that you should do very little (or no) athletic exercise on the days that you fast. You see, your "Fast Day" is the day you set aside to give your mind and body a rest. You don't have to stay in bed all day or anything like that but you really should take it easy both physically AND mentally.

What I do on my fast days is sort of kick back and read and putter around and, also, I have found it a good time to take care of those nagging little chores and errands that seem to accumulate during the rest of the week.

In other words, I think you should do road work every morning to more or less "order your day" and fast every week in order to "order your week."

You know what, son? I am 46 years and one day old, and the two things I have written to you about so far are the most important things I have ever learned.

And just think. You can start right now before you are even 16 years old. God, what a head start you will have!

Now, let's go on. The next thing I want to talk to you about is your diet. First of all, I believe that everybody who says breakfast is the most important meal of the day is dead wrong. In my opinion, all you should eat before lunch is a couple pieces of fruit. Do you remember what I said to you in yesterday's letter? I said you should eat a piece of fruit (preferably a banana) before you start your road work.

Well, after your road work, in my judgment, what you should do is take a shower, clean up, and get dressed and get your day started. And then, sometime after that, before lunch, you should eat another piece of fruit. Actually, you should eat three pieces of fruit every day (except when you fast) and I think you can't miss with a banana, an apple, or an orange. This way, you will get your potassium and your vitamims (and something called pectin, all of which is very good for you!).

Incidentally, I have read, and I believe it to be true, that fruit is the prize food of man. Also, I believe that fruit is perhaps the number one food category that Americans need to eat more of.

Watch your Mom. Watch other people. How much fruit do they eat? Very little I'll bet, and they are missing out on something very, very important.

One reason, of course, is that fruit contains a lot of stuff that is good for you and, another reason is fruit, along with certain other foods, acts sort of like "nature's broom" and helps keep you cleaned out and mobilating.

Anyway, as I said yesterday, I'm just warming up right now and I intend to write more on all this at a later date. But for now, it would be an excellent idea if you would start eating three pieces of fruit everyday, and start right after you get this letter.

You know Bond, in addition to everything else, you are the best student I have ever had and it is a real joy to teach all these things to you. Boy, I sure wish my dad had been able to do this for me, but that's water over the dam.

But maybe we can start a tradition here. A new "Halbert Tradition" whereupon the fathers make it a point to pass down what they have learned to teach a new generation.

It would be nice.

Okay, here's more info on the subject of diet. What else should you eat? Well, one thing is sure: You should definitely eat a big bowl of some "bran type" cereal. Grapenuts is probably the best you can find in an ordinary grocery store, and some health food stores have cereals that are even better.

By the way, remember yesterday when I asked you to get a copy of "The Joy Of Running"? Well, here are two other books you should look for: "The Miracle of Fasting" by Paul Bragg and "Are You Confused?" by Paulo Airola. Many health food stores will probably carry both of these books.

By the way, I don't want you to feel like you have to write to me as much as I am writing to you. I do want to hear from you (and often) but you are not writing a book like I am so no guilt trips are necessary.

Let's take a break and talk about something else. There's an old tomcat around here at the camp named Crackers. Crackers is an arrogant cat. There is a lot of small game around here and Crackers like to catch these little critters and plays with them.

For example, a week or so ago, I was doing my morning road work and I spotted Crackers as I was coming down the backside of "The Hill." Crackers had a little critter in his mouth that looks just like a baby chipmunk. These little guys are cute as hell and I have since (I'm getting tired) found out that they are, in reality, Antelope Ground Squirrels.

Anyway, Crackers had this cute little creature in his mouth and he brought it over to me and then dropped it. The critter just laid there. Then, after a little while, Crackers would bat it around a little with his front paws. After a while, the critter began to stir and then it tried to run away. Crackers caught it again in short order and began to repeat the whole process. What I mean is that he would carry it in his mouth and then drop it and then torment it until finally the poor thing had no fight left.

In other words, Crackers just messed with this little squirrel until he tormented the life out of it. And then, after all this, do you know what else he would do? What he would do is pick up the squirrel again in his mouth and toss his head back and throw it up in the air and then bat it back and forth while it was in the air like he was playing handball with it.

Whatever. In any case, when I told some other inmate about this he said, "Yeah, but that stupid Crackers is nothing but a stupid punk. He always takes trash from the other cats around here. There's a black cat from over at the housing area that whips him all the time!"

What's the point of all this? Probably, there isn't one but it reminds me of something I read once in an article in "The Herald Examiner" in which someone was quoted as saying:

"There is no justice. There is only power."

That's it for now.

<u>I Love You and Good Luck!</u>
Dad
7:07 P.M.

*(Sorry, but that is how inmates talk.)

UPDATE:

In this second letter, Pop begins by remarking on his new get-tough attitude and with all due respect, that is total bullshit. He was ALWAYS tough. I have no illusions about my father, and he was not tough in all situations and certainly had his fears as we all do, but in general he has always been tough.

He grew up in an economically depressed small town, served as an MP in Germany and had five children by the time he was thirty. He got rich, went broke, got rich and blew it all again several times by this point in his life and squarely faced going to prison head on.

Oh, he carried fear for sure, but he always did what he had to and he faced some tough shit.

The hidden point he might make if he re-read the letter today would be how he hates mean people. Cruelty was something he hated to his core and once he knew someone was scum, he developed a hardcore tough attitude towards that person.

This was an important survival skill. In life, everyone must learn to deal with unnecessary grief from other people, but sometimes you are faced with a jerk who has the balance of power in their favor, and the only way to survive, especially with your pride intact, is to develop a mental toughness as a form of mental armor. Once you do…. that attitude is always there when you really need it.

The people who ran Boron didn't inspire a new get-tough attitude in him. No… they simply inspired his toughness to surface.

On the subject of fasting, I did try it a few times shortly after receiving this letter, but I hate fasting.

However, his letters did inspire me to eat more fruit than most other people of my generation and all of his nutritional advice in the letters is spot on.

As I said in the first commentary, my father abused his body, went on health kicks and yet, he died at 67 so it is impossible to judge how much he extended his own life. He did manage to make it 10 more years than his father but…

After he passed, the medical examiner remarked that he was in great shape, other than being dead of course. He would have loved that comment.

Seriously though, she did say he was in terrific shape other than his blocked artery and enlarged heart which seems to be hereditary in origin.

Before we get far from the subject of fasting, he made what I believe to be the most overlooked lesson of the letter and that was when he wrote, "don't tell anyone."

My dad's favorite saying was "nothing is impossible for a man who refuses to listen to reason," and it served him well his whole life.

He did so many things other people said couldn't be done. This shouldn't be taken as "never listen to reasonable people", but just because someone *says* you can't do something or shouldn't, doesn't mean they are right, even if the whole world agrees with them.

Most of the people in the world are nay-sayers. They say it is too hard to quit smoking or it is too tough to get rich or you will never make it. When it comes to accomplishing things, most people fail to even try. There is no benefit in dealing with people who have nothing but negative things to say. When that someone amounts to just about everyone, just keep it to yourself.

This reminds me of the Australian doctor who discovered a non-surgical cure for ulcers. Everyone in the scientific community agreed that no viruses or anything could live in the acidic conditions inside the human stomach. He spent a LOT of time trying to convince other doctors he was right. Finally, he ignored all of them and went about his research and proved that most ulcers are caused by organisms in the stomach.

He Had To Treat & <u>Cure</u> Several People
Before The Medical Community Would
Pay Attention To Him!

But he sure would have saved a lot of time by not bothering to argue and just finishing his work.

All people KNEW the world was flat and the sun revolved around it, and what happened when people offered up a different idea? They were punished for heresy and ridiculed by their colleagues.

No, sometimes there is no use wasting time and energy fighting established beliefs by arguing, and it is better to just silently go about proving or accomplishing your goal.

Finally, in this letter, he touches briefly on the idea that I would continue to pass on and add any wisdom to my kids' early development. This was written 15 years before my first child Emma Rose was born.

Other than in this letter, I don't recall him ever talking about me writing letters until one day I told him what I was doing.

He was very proud that I decided to write letters to my kids, and he really knew how much I appreciate what he had done for me.

Anyway, the last part of the letter is about Crackers. I remember Crackers and he didn't strike me as any more smug than most house cats, but Pop really liked the ground squirrels.

The Boron Letters
Chapter 3

Thursday, 3:26 p.m.
June 14, 1984

Dear Bond,

Guess what?

Today I jogged "The Hill" two times without stopping!

Big deal, huh? Well, it is to me. Your old man is getting lean and mean.

Anyway, let's get started. First of all, I want to briefly review what I have suggested to you so far.

1. I have suggested that you do one hour's worth of road work every morning right after you get up for six days a week.

2. I have suggested you eat three pieces of fruit every day.
3. I have suggested you eat a large bowl of some bran type cereal every day.

Now, let's go from there. What else should your daily diet consist of? Well, for one thing, you should eat a lot of vegetables. What I suggest is that you get yourself some kind of baggie or plastic container, and every night before you go to sleep, I suggest you cut up a bunch of new veggies and put them in the container and then put the container in the refrigerator. Then, in the morning, when you are ready to leave the house, you can grab your raw veggies and take them with you to munch on them all day.

By the way, don't listen to all that garbage that says you should not eat between meals. You should eat between meals. In fact, six small meals is a lot better than three big ones. Actually, what is best is to have a little nibble whenever you get hungry. And this is a good way to eat your vegetables. Just carry your container with you wherever you go and eat some whenever you get hungry.

Incidentally, this is a habit that will go a long way in keeping you from feeling tired because it will tend to keep your blood sugar level at a more or less constant level.

WARNING! Don't depend on your mother or anybody else to buy or cut up your vegetables for you. You should, instead, develop a tough independent attitude.

You see, when you depend on others, you give yourself an excuse for failure. "It's not my fault if she forgot to buy my vegetables." And so on. Don't set yourself up like this. Depend on yourself.

O.K. So far, we've got you eating fruit, vegetables and a bran type cereal. What else? Well, one thing else I think you should do is drink one large glass of non-fat milk every day. This will give you your calcium, some protein, and some other good stuff.

And, what else? More protein, of course. As I said, you'll get some protein from your milk but it won't be nearly enough. You should also have at least one serving of some kind of lean meat or fowl.

Hamburgers are fine too.

Go easy on eggs. Two or three a week is plenty. They contain a lot of cholesterol and that's the stuff (along with fats) that can clog up your arteries.

Here's a couple more good ideas. (1) Buy yourself a box of bran flakes and mix two or three heaping tablespoons full into your cereal or whatever. (2) Get some protein powder. You can get this at most any health food store and I now believe it is a good idea (especially for a growing boy) to add some protein powder to his diet every day as "protein insurance."

What else should you eat? Actually, just about anything you want. I think it is a bad idea to ever forbid yourself to ever have ice cream or a soft drink or whatever. Just go easy and use a little common sense.

But don't worry. You see, if you keep up your road work and eat all the foods you should eat every day, you won't have much room (or much inclination) to load yourself up with junk.

Let's take a break. I'm going to stop writing in a minute or two anyway because it is time for mail call. You know, Bondo, I've been thinking. I figure it will take me about one hundred letters to teach you the basics of what I want you to know. This should come out to between 500 to 1,000 legal pages of writing, and these pages will form the core or nucleus of the book I want to write.

After I get this first part done, I intend to take notes from various good books on exercise, diet, selling by mail, etc. and then, at this point, I should be able to sit down with all these letters and notes and then outline the book I want to write. After that, I'll write the first draft of the book. Then, after that, I'll review everything all over again and then write the final draft. I figure my timetable for the book to work out roughly like this:

1. Letters to Bond 3-months

2. Notes from other books .. 2-months

3. Outline .... 1-month (maximum)

4. First draft 2-months

5. Final draft .... 1-1/2 months

6. Polish .... 1-1/2 months

Total ... 11-MONTHS

Remember - these are very rough estimates. Actually, it is my goal to have the book finished after about ten months of solid work, which means I should (hopefully) be done by middle of next April.

We'll see. But one thing is true. This is the best place to write and get healthy I've ever been. I seem to get more productive every day.

Maybe, I'll have to commit some new federal crime every couple of years in order to get my books done!

Just kidding. Just kidding.

Strange. We usually have the mail by now but today it is late.

Oh well, I'll just keep writing.

STOP 4:14

Start Again 4:25

I was interrupted by mail call and now they are having "count." Count is simply when they count us to make sure we are all here.

They do this often.

Whatever. I was about to say let's get back to business. Now that I have (hopefully) got you doing your morning road work and eating more or less properly, I want to talk about other exercise in addition to road work.

Actually, I don't think I have to say a lot right now because you are probably doing just fine at Questar.

As I keep saying, I'm just warming up right now and I'll cover exercise in more detail later. But anyway, right now, I just want to say that I want you to concentrate on developing your arms.

All you really have to do are presses and curls. You know, I don't think it is desirable to have a body builder's body. Women, in general, are not attracted to the exaggerated development of body builders and I personally don't like this type of physique either.

I think a man looks best (and I think most women would agree with me) when he is lean an hard - not bulging and overdeveloped.

However, I do think it is a good idea to spend enough time to develop strong muscular arms.

There are two reasons for this. First, of all, it is useful to be strong. Secondly, I think women are attracted to lean, hard men with strong muscular arms. And, thirdly, from a prison point of view, just having big arms can keep you out of a lot of trouble, I'll discuss this in more detail tomorrow.

Bye for now,

I LOVE YOU AND GOOD LUCK!

Gary 4:37 PM

UPDATE:

This third letter appears to cover only health suggestions, but there are also two business lessons to be learned, and one is in no way evident.

The advice on health and working out is again very good and I agree with it, so there is very little to add, but...

The part where he tells me not to rely on anyone is a whole lesson all by itself.

By this point, you can see my father had a healthy disdain for the mindset of regular people, and that is indeed a positive attribute especially when it comes to making money.

When most people tell others of any plan to make money, they are met with instant negativity.

Once you set out to actually do something which may elevate your status, many people will tell you it can't be done, it isn't worth it, or remind you of all the pitfalls they can think of.

I don't care what you think of your friends or family, it is in most people's nature to stop you. Don't get the idea that this is in everything you attempt, just when you attempt to do things on a scale so grand that if successful, you will be a whole lot richer than they are.

Again, people don't do this consciously. It's simply a self-defense mechanism to make themselves feel better because

The Idea of You Getting Rich Makes Most People Around You Feel Sick!

Let's suppose you come up with the idea to open the first biodiesel fuel station in Barstow, the small town almost exactly half way between Los Angeles and Las Vegas. As you begin to explain how you can obtain financing and get equipment, they will immediately tell you how regulation and property prices are obstacles. They will say these problems are insurmountable and are too hard to overcome.

One logical assumption is that people do this because they obviously are people with a CAN'T do attitude, but that doesn't explain people who own their own businesses putting ideas down and they often do. I think it is because your peers translate your success into their failure for not becoming rich.

Let's face it, most people judge how well they have done in life by comparing themselves to their peers, and if one of their peers has become a multi-millionaire and could retire young and rich, then they will have to question their own choices.

It is ironic that so many people say they want to be rich, yet they put down almost everyone who tries, and often they put down those that do succeed.

There is an irrational hatred of the rich and it is born out of spite. Terms like "filthy rich" and "born with a silver spoon in the mouth" are not compliments. You can worry about that when you are rich, but for now you need to worry about all those people who want to stop you from becoming rich.

Just remember where they are coming from and try to surround yourself with people who have similar goals or who have already become great successes. These people are almost always hungry for people to appreciate what they have accomplished and like to be recognized for more than the size of their bank account.

For anyone who thinks their friends and family will support them no matter what their goal is, tell them you plan to open a restaurant. They will tell you more than 90% of new restaurants fail within one minute. They will never say, "a lot dumber people than you have opened great restaurants, so go for it."

Ever notice that almost everyone knows that stat yet can't quote current money market returns? Our schools teach people how to work within businesses, but never how to start a business. Is it better to teach your kids how to change oil in the car or how to write an ad to bring in business? It is almost as if we have all been trained to accept capitalism, but only as part of the workforce.

Anyway, it is vital that you never let the bastards get you down, and in this case, the bastards are almost everyone you meet.

The other point which I feel can be made now is that he repeats himself often. This is not absent mindedness and is 100% intentional.

This lesson is much like the one in the previous letter.

It is widely accepted and both my dad and I agreed that one of the best business books in the world is The Godfather. My dad often remarked on how he loved the book and film. One of his favorite lessons in the book was when the Godfather explains to his youngest son Michael that he must continue to think about and go over their plans for the future.

In the film, Brando says to Pacino, "I hope you don't mind me going over this Barzini business," and then explains he does it to avoid being careless. Going over and over plans is a good way to make sure everyone is on the same page and remembers small things.

Write down your goals and go over them every day, not just once a year.

The Boron Letters
Chapter 4

Friday, 11:05 AM
June 15, 1984

Dear Bond,

It was very nice for all of you to come up yesterday and bring me a birthday cake. It is good to know that you are all on my side and that I have a strong outside "support system."

I hope everybody understood why I wanted to leave before 7:30. If I hadn't left when I did, I would have missed commissary and I wouldn't have gotten my supply of fruit for the whole week. Also, Doc, my best friend in Boron so far, was leaving the next morning (that's this morning; he's gone now) and I needed to spend more time with him.

But I do appreciate all of you and I just wanted to let you know.

Onward. Let's get back to the subject of physique. As I said yesterday, I believe the best physique for a man is lean and hard with strong muscular arms but not a bulging, exaggerated weight-lifter's body.

But why do I stress arm development so much? There are several reasons. As I said yesterday, one benefit is that it is just plain handy to have a lot of strength in your arms. I also said the kind of body I have been touting is attractive to women and wins you respect from men.

Let's talk about that respect a little bit. The first thing I want to say is that a fat, sloppy, or skinny and weak body tends to broadcast to the world that the owner of that body is lacking self-respect. The second thing is that tough animals have a tendency to prey on weak or helpless animals.

Here is something to remember: DEFENSIVE BEHAVIOR INVITES AGGRESSIVE ACTION

What that means is that in life in general (and in prison in particular), there is very little sympathy for a weakling.

There's a guy here that I used to like, but now he is starting to irritate me. In many ways he's nice old guy (I'll write more about him later), but he is serving a miserable 100 day sentence (maybe it's even less) and he shuffles around like a plantation nigger trying to please "Ol Massah." What's going on is plain and simple: He's scared.

Now, that's no sin. God knows I've been scared many times. But this guy stays scared when there is no need to be, and it is very unattractive to watch.

Now, don't get the wrong idea and start worrying about this guy. I am very nice to him and so is everybody else. Everybody cuts him a lot of slack. This is a very "soft" place to do your time and all I want to do by describing this man's mode of behavior to you is to make a point.

The point is this: Bond, as you know, I am a very non-violent person and if this guy, by acting like such a pussy, can irritate me, just think how some hard vicious hard-nosed jerk in a real prison would be affected by him!

You see, this guy is sending out signals and those signals are saying, *"I'm scared. I'm a pussy. I'm easy. I'm vulnerable."* And so on.

And, unfortunately, not everybody in the world is kind or sympathetic. Some men just look for guys like this guy to prey on.

God, I'm long-winded aren't I? Anyway, finally to get to the point, what I'm trying to say is that it is far better to:

**rely on your own strength
instead of somebody else's
compassion!**

And, to make the obvious point, you've obviously first got to have some strength in order to be able to rely on it.

You can't fake it. At least it's not a good idea. Especially in a prison or anywhere else where there are "mean streets." You don't need to "act tough," you need to be tough.

Don't get me wrong. I'm not talking about being mean or macho or even pushy. I'm also not talking about pumping iron for hours a day or getting a black belt in karate either.

You don't have to do all that. Plain simple toughness will do. You see most predators, when it comes to their victims, are very practical. Let's face it. If a couple of guys decide to go to the park and mug somebody, they aren't going to pick on some big gnarly looking guy. No, they will go after the victim who looks like easy pickup.

STOP 11:43

START AGAIN 7:17 PM

You know what? I believe that if you have two guys of the same height and same weight, and you dress them both in a full suit of clothes, that most of the time, you will still be able to tell who is the toughest. You see, when you "get tough," not only does your appearance change, your "signals" change also. The way you move, the way you hold yourself, your reactions to outside stimuli - all of that changes.

So I want you to start getting tough and self-reliant. By the way, I read a quote by John D. Rockefeller in "The Enquirer" today to the effect that nothing is as satisfying as self-reliance, and I totally agree.

But don't get confused. I don't want you to become a fighter in the physical sense as much as I want you to become a "Fight Avoider." I want you to be able to avoid fights without losing your dignity.

One of the best ways to avoid fights (I know this sounds kind of silly!) is to have big arms. Have you ever heard this comment? *"Damn! Look at the arms on that guy! How'd you like to meet him in a dark alley?!"*

Big strong arms. Start developing them right now. There are no drawbacks and many benefits.

Well, hopefully, by now I've got you doing your road work, developing your arms and eating more or less properly. On that assumption I am going to temporarily drop this area and start writing about how to make money. We'll come back to health and fitness later though.

But tomorrow we'll start on money. However, right now, I want to comment briefly on one of my friends here. He is black and he was formerly in San Quentin for shooting two Santa Monica cops because he thought they were trying to get his supply of dope.

He's a heroin dealer from Hollywood and he is 55 years old and he is indeed a "career criminal." He thought she was going to OD from the heroin he had sold her. He's a fascinating guy and maybe we'll talk about him at another time.

Some guy was taken out of his hand cuffs yesterday. They found a bunch of money and pot in his hobby shop locker. Last night, my friend Doc told me a story about this guy. It seems that some guy snitched on him and his wife and caused his wife to go to jail.

Well, anyway, for some reason, this guy was in another institution. He was part of a line of guys who were handcuffed and in chains when he spotted the snitch.

What does he do? Simple. He grabs a nearby pencil (or pen, I forget) and tries to ram it into the snitch's brain by stabbing him in the eye. As it turned out, he didn't kill the snitch, but he did manage to blind him.

What the hell. It was just "his way."

I'm going to sign off now. Are you following my suggestions?

I love you and Good Luck!

Love Dad
7:42 PM

UPDATE:
The beginning seems like a simple "sorry for cutting everything so short last time" sentence to his family and it was, but it really says a whole lot more.

You can see how nothing stood in the way of what Gary felt was important to his life and to sticking to his routine. He really did prioritize well and had insane focus.

This remark really does show his appreciation for a good support system. Everyone knows a good group of folks behind you can be REALLY helpful. Look at men of average skills who attain lofty positions for no better reason than the other people who help them out.

That being said....my dad had a rare and enviable ability to eradicate people from his life if they were not a positive influence.

We all have people in our lives we feel like we are stuck dealing with for a variety of reasons loyalty based on past friendship, family, or some other sense of duty. Well not my pop. He said SCREW THAT and if someone didn't add to his enjoyment, he would cut them right out of his life for good.

He wasn't mean, but he just wouldn't put up with nonsense from ANYONE! My brother Kevin is like that, and I try to learn from them both because it makes a lot of difference to one's success.

Imagine if everyone you deal with is really on your side and not only believes in you, but they all also want to seriously help you accomplish your goals.

Most people think the hard part is finding positive people, but that isn't true. Go to any learning annex workshop with Trump speaking and you will find positive people with hope. No, the real trick is to cut out those that hold you back.

The first person to try and hold my dad back was his own father. On several occasions, my dad told me of how my grandfather told him he wouldn't be able to breakout of the average working Joe's existence.

Grandpa had such a lack of faith in upward mobility that when my dad actually did strike it rich, his dad simply wouldn't believe it until my dad showed him mailbags full of checks from people wanting to buy his reports. This was all AFTER my dad bought a new custom home in the nicest part of town and built a huge business.

Once my dad stopped seeking his father's approval, he realized he was in control of his own destiny. Without being malicious…. he started to marginalize the people that held him back.

He sent some money to his mom whenever she needed anything, but for the most part, we moved to California and my grandparents became a much smaller part of our lives.

He even wrote about this in "The Dark Side Of Success."

He would never want me to tarnish the name of anyone in the family by citing examples, but suffice it to say, he had the ability and more importantly the WILL to eliminate or marginalize anyone in his life he felt was too negative.

Most of us like to think we would do the same, but we always have an excuse. "So-and-so is my in-law so I can't tell him to piss up a rope, "or" we have been friends since high school." Screw that.

Never, ever encourage people who drag you down to hang around.

A support system is like a garden, and you always need to be on the lookout for weeds to pull.

The other lesson in this chapter is don't be or appear to be a weak target. He discusses having large arms as a deterrent and he is 100% right.

Right before my dad went in to prison, a friend of mine commented that he wouldn't mess with my dad. The comment struck me as odd because I saw my dad as one big, loveable guy of average height, and my friend had just kicked his mom's boyfriend's ass about a week earlier.

I asked him why he thought so and his answer was, "his arms." His arms weren't huge like a body builder, but you could tell they were strong, proving the point my dad would later be making in this fourth letter.

In business, my father tried to never appear weak, and it is easier to not appear weak when you are strong. If he found out someone was charging more for an ad, he raised his price. He was the best and he was putting it out there. Carry yourself with confidence (not arrogance) in everything you do and people will respond in a good way.

He ends the letter with a quote by Rockefeller that self-reliance is the most satisfying thing in the world. It is important to know that often, self-reliance is the real motive of great business men and not money.

The Boron Letters
Chapter 5

Saturday, 10:02 a.m.
June 16, 1984

Dear Bond,

 How's my favorite youngest son? I'm sitting here waiting for the phone and I decided to start writing so let's push forward.

 Today, we are going to get started on the subject of how to make money. Usually, when someone asks me what is the #1 big secret to making money, I tell them they should get involved in whatever excites them the most.

 This is good advice. Money, in my opinion, especially big money, is most often a by-product of enthusiasm. If a person, secretly in his heart, wants to be an architect, he shouldn't go into selling real estate, for example, just because he has heard that that is where the money is.

 The money is where the enthusiasm is. Please remember this! Remember it also, when, in the future, you need to hire someone. Always look for the most enthusiastic person, not necessarily the most qualified.

 When it comes to making money, attitude is the most important thing of all. That's why you are so appreciated at Advanced Management. You have <u>exactly</u> the kind of attitude that a sharp employer looks for. So remember all this and when it is your turn

STOP APPROX 10:11

START AGAIN
10:27

to hire someone. Usually, Bond, when I discuss making money with someone, I spend a lot more time on attitude because it is so important. But you <u>already</u> have a <u>great</u> attitude so I'll save any further discussion for later.

 Also, you already seem to have a natural talent and enthusiasm for direct marketing so I am going to directly proceed to that area.

 Now, pay attention. The very first thing you must come to realize is that you must become a "student of markets." Not products. Not techniques. Not copywriting. Not how to buy space or whatever. Now, of course, all of these things are important and you must learn about them, but, the first and the most important thing you must learn is what people want to buy.

And it's easy. You see, the way to deduce what people want to buy is to simply observe what they DO buy!

It's as simple as that. But be careful. You want to know what people actually DO buy, not what they SAY they buy.

Here's a true story. Once upon a time, a beer company did a survey to find out which of their products customers preferred. You know what? To their astonishment, they found that 80% or so of the people they surveyed preferred their premium beer as opposed to their regular beer.

Why were they astonished? The answer is easy. You see, their sales figures were showing that most people bought their regular beer and NOT the premium.

What's going on here? Well, for one thing, it is very common. You see, the surveyed people were trying to give the "right" answer and so they put down as an answer the beer they felt they SHOULD DRINK.

It happens all the time. But pity any poor fool who decides to go into the brewery business based on this kind of erroneous marketing information.

Here's another example of how people struggle to give the "right" answer. How many people do you know who read the National Enquirer? Not many huh? Almost everybody I talk with really puts down the Enquirer (even here in Boron). But guess what? The "National Enquirer" is the largest selling newspaper in the world - BY FAR!

Yet nobody reads it. At least not here on Earth. It must be all those Martians.

What do people read? I'll bet if you took a survey, you would discover that the most read book of all is the Bible.

It's just not true. Hardly anyone (percentage wise) has actually read the Bible. A lot of people own a Bible, a lot of people DISPLAY their Bibles, some people are given to swearing on a Bible but damn few people have actually READ the Bible.

And who can blame them? The Bible is repetitive, hard-to-read and most of it all is deadly boring.

Yet people feel guilty and, in their attempt to give the RIGHT answer, they will say (and often convince themselves) that the Bible is their favorite reading material.

You want to know what some people would consider a sickening statistic? Here it is: MORE PEOPLE READ THE "NATIONAL ENQUIRER" IN ONE SINGLE WEEK THAN HAVE EVER READ THE BIBLE IN THE LAST 2,000 YEARS!

Sorry. But that's the way it is. And, if you want to be a top notch marketing man, you have to know how it is. How it really is. Not how people (or you) wish it was or how they think it is. No. You must become a "student of reality."

How do you find out what people actually buy? And, more particularly, how do you find out what they buy via direct response? The "SRDS Direct Mail List Book." Then what you should do is turn to the CONSUMER LISTS section and just start reading. It will be quite an adventure. You should pay special attention to the numbers involved and the descriptions of the lists.

Let's see if I can find an example. Aha! Here are a few that look very interesting under section 561 which is the classification for INVESTORS.

Diamond And Ruby Buyers

Description: Investment counselors,
brokers, dealers and individuals
who have purchased diamonds and rubies.

AVERAGE UNIT OF SALE   = $5,000.00

QUANTITY   =   3,979

Wow! Let's think about this for a minute. Here are almost 4,000 people who, according to this information have spent an average of $5,000.00 to buy diamonds and rubies. Let's see now... $5,000 apiece times 4,000 buyers equals - uh 20 MILLION DOLLARS!

Think about it. What else would they be likely to buy? How about more of the same? (That's usually a good bet.) Maybe (probably) they'd be receptive to a hot new diamond offer.

Hmm?

Here's another:

Diamond Buyers And Enquirers

Description: People who purchased
or inquired about purchasing
diamonds. 60% buyers.
AVERAGE UNIT OF SALE   = $5,000.00

(always pay special attention to the average unit of sale - the higher the better!)

QUANTITY   =   52,000

Let's do the numbers on this one:

52,000 x 60% buyers = 31,200 actual buyers... and...

31,200 buyers x $5,000 comes to:

ONE HUNDRED AND FIFTY SIX
MILLION DOLLARS

Hot damn! Figures like that will get your greed glands going won't they?

                                        Stop 11:30

                                        More later.
                                    I Love You and
                                        Good Luck!

                                                Dad

P.S. Believe it or not, I didn't know about the above lists until just now. I really and truly turned to them totally by accident. Isn't that something?

UPDATE:
The SRDS is still a great tool and has an online division but I'd like to make the case that space ads and direct mail pieces enjoy little competition and great pricing.

With everyone looking for free exposure and JVs, it's often the guys who invest actual money who make the big bucks and they don't brag about it either.

Anyway, you can contact the SRDS (Standard Rate and Data Service) online at:
http://next.srds.com/home

The Boron Letters
Chapter 6

Sunday, 10:16 a.m.
June 17, 1984

Dear Bond,

No messing around. I'm going to dive right back into the subject of becoming a "student of markets."

As you know, once in a while, I give a class on copywriting and/or selling by mail. One of the questions I like to ask my students is: *"If you and I both owned a hamburger stand and we were in a contest to see who would sell the most hamburgers, what advantages would you most like to have on your side?"*

The answers vary. Some people say they would like to have the advantage of having superior meat from which to make their hamburgers. Others say they want sesame seed buns. Others mention location. Someone usually wants to be able to offer the lowest prices.

And so on.

Anyway, after my students are finished telling what advantages they would most like to have, I say to them: *"O.K., I'll give you every single advantage you asked for. I, myself, only want one advantage and, if you will give it to me, I will whip the pants off of all of you when it comes to selling burgers!"*

"What advantage do you want?" they ask.

"The only advantage I want," I reply, *"is A STARVING CROWD!"*

What I am trying to teach you here is to constantly be on the lookout for groups of people (markets) who have demonstrated that they are starving (or at least hungry!) for some particular product or service.

How do you measure this hunger? Well, fortunately, if you are working with mailing lists, it is rather easy. Let's take an example: Suppose you want to sell a book on how to invest money and you have created a direct mail promotion designed to sell this book. Who do you mail your promotion to? Here are some possibilities:

Possibility #1 - We could mail it to people whose names and address we get right out of a telephone book.

   Comments: This is a terrible idea. There are too many non-prospects in this kind of group. The only thing in common that people in the phone book have is that they all have a phone. Some of the people won't have any money to invest. Some of them never purchase anything by mail. Some of them are too busy (or uninterested) to even read your letter. Some of them don't even know how to read! In short, there is too much waste circulation. This is like shooting with a shotgun instead of a rifle.

   Onward.

Possibility #2 - We could mail our promotion to people whose names and addresses we get from a phone book, but only to those people who live in high income areas.

   Comments: This is a little better, but not nearly good enough. High income areas are, incidentally, easy to identify because several companies have compiled statistics on every zip code in the United States. They can tell you with great accuracy the average income per person in each zip code. They can also, by the way, tell you the average education level, average age, how much they spend on automobiles, and a bunch of other stuff.

   However, as I said, this still isn't nearly good enough. For one thing, not everybody who lives in a high-income area has a high income. Some of these people might be the maids or gardeners or some other type of servant. (Come to think of it, I'm not so sure that quite a few gardeners aren't wealthy.) Some of these people may have money but are not interested in investing. Some of them may always buy books from a bookstore and never by mail. Some of these people can't read English. (There are more and more rich foreigners in our country.) Some of them may have money to invest but are only interested in investing in areas in which they already have expertise.

   Whatever. Once again we are shooting with a shotgun instead of a rifle. Once again, too much waste circulation.

   Let's see if we can do a little better.

Possibility #3 - We could mail our piece to a group of people that we are relatively sure have above average incomes. Like doctors. Lawyers. Architects. Top executives. Accountants. Owners of expensive homes. Owners of Rolls Royce automobiles.

   And so on.

<u>Comments</u>: Not bad. We are now getting into areas where we at least have a chance.

STOP
11:01 AM

START AGAIN
6:52 PM

At least we are relatively sure that most of these people have a high enough income to maybe be interested in investing. Whether they are interested or not, we can't know, but at least if they are, they probably have the <u>ability</u> to do some investing. This group of people is certainly more likely to respond to our pitch than the first two groups but, as you shall see, we can do a lot better.

Possibility #4 - We could mail our promotion to a list of upper income people who are proven mail order buyers. Buyers of what, you ask? Actually, for the purposes of selling by mail, it is generally true that mail order buyers of <u>anything</u> are better than almost any group of non-mail order buyers. And, in this case, we have added the extra qualifications that they must be <u>wealthy</u> mail order buyers.

<u>Comments</u>: Now we are getting down to business. This is the first group I have described that gives us a reasonable shot at success. Not bad. Not bad at all. But now, let's stop fooling around and go for the hill!

Possibility #5 - We could mail our promotion to a group of wealthy people who have ordered some other investment book by mail.

<u>Comments</u>: Bingo! Now we're cooking. What could be better? They are upper income. They are mail order buyers. And, they have purchased BY MAIL a product similar to ours. What could be better? This is just about as "hot" of a list as we can get! Or is it? Actually, it is not. Let's keep trying.

Possibility #6 - We could mail our promotion to a list of wealthy people who have purchased (by mail) a product similar to ours - <u>several times</u>!

<u>Comments</u>: Yeah! Now we're cooking! Just imagine. They're MO buyers. They're wealthy! They've purchased (by mail) a product similar to ours. AND they are <u>repeat</u> buyers of this type of product. How sweet it is! Can it get any sweeter? Yes, dear son, it can! Read on.

Possibility #7 - We could mail our promotion to a list of wealthy people who have purchased (by mail) a product similar to ours - several times AND WHO HAVE PAID BIG MONEY FOR WHAT THEY BOUGHT.

Comments: Goody. These people are very close to the "crème de la crème" of lists we can mail to. But wait! Why do I say they are "very close" to the best? After all, what more could we ask for? Hold on! We're not done yet.

But not quite. Just keep reading.

Possibility #8 - We could mail our promotion to a list of wealthy people who have purchased (by mail) a product similar to ours - and who have done so repeatedly - and who have paid big money for what they purchased - AND WHO HAVE <u>VERY RECENTLY</u> MADE SUCH A PURCHASE!

Comments: This is almost as good a list as we can get. It is certainly the best list we are likely to be able to rent.

But not quite. Just keep reading.

Possibility #9 - We could mail our promotion to a list of people who have all the characteristics of possibility #8 AND WHO OUR FRIENDLY LIST BROKER TELLS US IS WORKING LIKE CRAZY FOR OTHER MAILERS WITH PROMOTIONS SIMILAR TO OURS.

Comments: For a variety of reasons, many lists that should work don't. Who knows why? It really doesn't matter why. What matters is that a list is or is not

STOP
7:25

START AGAIN
8:34

responsive. And the best way to know what lists are hot is to have a good relationship with a good honest broker. In fact, if you have a good relationship with a good broker, one of the things he will do (because it is to his financial advantage) is to keep an eye out for hot lists that are likely to work for your offers. And now, with this last list we have finally and truly identified the best list you can mail to.

Almost.

Yep. We can still do better!

Possibility #10 - There is one group of people who will respond even better than all the other 9 groups I have described. Can you guess what list this will be? Think about it a minute and then turn the page for the answer.

THE BEST LIST OF ALL IS
YOUR OWN CUSTOMER LIST!

<u>Comments</u>: All other things being equal, your own customers should respond far better than any other list you can get. Of course there is one caveat. THEY MUST BE <u>SATISFIED</u> CUSTOMERS!

That's it for now.

I Love You and
Good Luck!

Dad
8:43 PM

UPDATE:

It's true you can get decent gains by tweaking various aspects of your sales funnel and even though little changes can lead to big profits, nothing will add to your bottom line as fast as selling something new to your existing customers and sourcing new prospects.

Having something to upsell customers will always beat trying to make your website look fresh and upgrading to 3d buy buttons.

The numbers show that little tweaks do make a difference, but they show there is far more money in adding to your product line and creating backend offers, which Gary will discuss a little later in letters.

The Boron Letters
Chapter 7

Monday, 10:30 AM
June 18, 1984

Dear Bond,

Let's get right back into the subject of becoming a student of markets, especially mailing lists.

My last letter gave you a beginning insight into what makes a list more responsive. Let's review a few conclusions we came to based on the data in yesterday's letter. You will remember, of course, that I said that, as a general rule, any list of proven mail order buyers will out perform any list of non-buyers.

Now, as another general rule, there are three main guidelines you can rely on when you are picking lists to test.

STOP 10:35

START AGAIN
10:36

These three guidelines are recency, frequency and unit of sale. A brief explanation follows:

Recency - The more recently a person has purchased (by mail) something similar to what you are selling, the more receptive he will be to your offer. Get 'em while they're hot! In fact, always check to see if the list you are interested in has "hotline buyers" and see if you can rent them before anybody else. Hotline buyers are the most recent buyers of all. Sometimes they will be 90-day hotline buyers or even 30-day hotline buyers. These names are extremely good prospects!

Frequency - The more often a person buys a particular item, the higher his desire for that type of production service. It just makes sense. If you are selling a book on skin diving and you can find a list of people who have purchased several other books on skin diving, then you know he is interested in the subject and will be a likely prospect to buy your book.

<u>Unit of sale</u> - Once again, we have a guideline that just plain makes sense. After all, a person who recently paid $100.00 for a bottle of diet pills is probably a hotter prospect for diet type products than a person who has only paid $10.00 for a bottle of diet pills.

You know, Bondo-Dog, people don't always put their money where their mouths are; but they do nearly always put out their money where their true desires are.

Recency, frequency and unit of sale: all good guidelines for evaluation of a mail order list. And, in my opinion, of the three guidelines, <u>RECENCY</u> is, by far, the most important of all.

Now, let's discuss some other ways of finding out what people like to purchase by mail. In addition to mailing lists, there are a number of so called "hot" mail order publications. These are the newspapers and magazines that mail order companies advertise in over and over. You should make it a point to discover what these publications are. Get copies of them and become very familiar with them. You should pay attention to their editorial content, and pay special attention to the mail order ads they carry.

STOP 10:55

START AGAIN
11:27

There is a newsletter out of New York City called the "Gallagher Report." This newsletter covers the world of advertising. Once each year they publish a special edition that lists all of the major magazines and ranks them by circulation.

You should get a copy of this special issue (ask Eric), and then get copies of the top 100 magazines. Go through them and find out which ones carry a lot of mail order ads.

STOP 11:31

START AGAIN
8:56 PM

I have just come in after visiting with you, Kevin, B. and Z and a digression at this point might be productive. Z, as I am sure you will agree, probably feels a certain sense of relief that, because of the circumstances, she has more or less gotten her own way in regards to her ad. It's really too bad. <u>Too bad for her</u>! You have just seen an excellent example of why I generally treat clients with an iron fist. Z pulled this same stunt when she had her other ads written (by other people) and the ads were miserable failures.

If I were on the street I would have handled this situation in a totally different way. In fact, after about 5 minutes I would have told her to get lost and that she either gets out of my face, or else she can write her own ad.

The lesson here concerns control. Can you imagine how disastrous it would be if a patient could tell his surgeon how to do the operation? Or, if an athlete could tell his coach how to do his job?

I could go on and on. But isn't it ridiculous! A client pays me big money to write an ad and then they want to tell me how to do it!

It happens all the time. But not with me. At least not when I am on the outside. You see, part of the reason I am in so much demand is that I am so hard-headed. Clients, although they would never admit it, most often feel relieved with someone who takes a "don't you dare mess with my copy" attitude.

As you know, I couldn't make a scene in the visiting room but you can be sure that the next time I talk with Z that I am going to quietly but firmly put a lot of pain in her brain.

Here's another illustration of the importance of control. When B. took me aside, one of the things he explained to me was that *(name deleted)* in Vegas wants to put the commissions into another project and delay paying me.

Now, here's the thing. *(Name deleted)* is one of the <u>good guys</u>. And, sadly, even the good guys have trouble living up to their agreements when it comes to money. That's one of the reasons I try to structure my deeds so that I get paid <u>often</u>. You see, when there is big money involved it is very hard for the clients to write those checks.

STOP 9:17

START AGAIN
9:20

And, what really makes it hard for the client is that he usually believes that he doesn't need you anymore since he already has the ad.

Ah, there's a lesson here but, also, I'm blowing off steam. Let's get back to becoming aware of markets. Right here, what I want to do is encapsulate one of Halbert's Rules of Marketing Success. It is:

Sell People What They
Want To Buy!

So obvious, so overlooked and so important.

Now one thing I haven't mentioned so far is that you want to be on the lookout for ads and direct mail pieces that you see over and over. What this means is that whomever is running the ad has hit a nerve.

And, a good way for you to make money is for you to hit that same nerve, only do it better.

But, and I know I'm being redundant, the most important thing to do first is to <u>locate</u> those hot buttons. You don't have to guess. You don't have to wonder. You don't have to ask people or take surveys.

All You Have To Do Is Observe!

Observe the ads that keep repeating. Observe the size of the mailing lists available for rental on different product areas.

Observe the direct mail pieces that keep getting mailed out month after month, and sometimes year after year.

More tomorrow.

I Love You and
Good Luck!

Dad
9:31

UPDATE:

Many people have said my father could sell ice to Eskimos, and it's meant to be a compliment, but that is the exact opposite of what he preached.

Gary Halbert felt the smartest marketers offer all the Eskimos a great deal on heaters!

So many people get excited about Gary Halbert's copywriting skill, they forget his main focus was on good hooks, offers and solutions.

My brother Kevin and I know far more about Gary Halbert-level copy than anyone else on Earth, but we don't focus on writing better copy. We focus on creating better deals.

We watched as people came from all over the world to learn how to write copy from Gary Halbert and after a few editing lessons and a couple homework exercises, he concentrated on teaching them how to become marketers.

He taught them to go after the low hanging fruit first.

Also, I'd like to add an observation to his point about getting paid often and how good people do bad things.

Some of my favorite people owe me money.

It doesn't matter that they can afford to pay me or even that they know they lost way more money in missed opportunities because I can't recommend or work with them.

It's basically a mental block people have to being able to hand over money unless they see an immediate payoff.

The larger the debt ,the larger their aversion to paying; so if one week's commission becomes two weeks owed, etc., the small debt starts to increase as you let it slide.

This is why you should try to get paid as often as possible and spell out simple agreements via email.

You could save a good relationship as well as a lot of money.

The Boron Letters
Chapter 8

Tuesday, 10:52 AM
June 19, 1984

Dear Bond,

  Another digression. I am tired. I was upset after last night's visit plus my roommate was snoring like a buzzsaw last night. (Poetic justice)

  Anyway, what should a person do when he is tired? Should he stay on his program, or should he rest? It all depends. I am skipping lunch today and I am writing this on my lunch hour. If it turns out, that in my opinion, I am just spinning my wheels, I will stop writing and start resting.

  The same applies to my road work which I will start a couple hours from now. You see, the way I look at it, if you halt your forward progress every time you get a little tired or irritable or whatever, then you are suffering from a lack of discipline. On the other hand, if you keep pushing when you are chronically tired or really sick, then you are a fool. A lot of men do this because of a misplaced sense of macho.

  It's not macho, it's stupid.

  So what I do when, like today, I don't feel like working, is that I start working anyway and I pay attention to what signals my brain and body is sending me. Then, after working a while, if I <u>honestly</u> do start to feel worse, I will stop and quit. However, if I just feel a little bit crummy (as I do now), I keep on plugging along.

  As someone once said, *"Most of the world's work is done by people who didn't feel much like getting out of bed."*

  So true.

  By the way, I am having coffee and V8 Juice. I am a big fan of V-8. It's cheap, it only has 36 calories, and, when you pour it over a tall glass of ice cubes, it really tastes great.

  Give it a try. It's a nice alternative once in a while to eating or having a soft drink.

  Now, back to marketing. You know, one of the remarks I hear all the time when I ask someone what they think of one of my ads goes something like this: *"Oh, I'm not a good person to ask. I never buy anything by mail."*

Really. Mail order sales run into the billions of dollars each year but rarely will you run into anyone who admits to being a mail order buyer.

Personally, I think all these "non-mail order buyers" are the same people who <u>don't</u> read the National Enquirer.

Once again, it must be all those Martian invaders.

What I am doing here is redundantly making a point, and I am going to be even more redundant. Here's another little glimpse into one of the vagaries of human behavior: Once I asked at class at USC how many of them preferred to go to plays more than movies.

Lots of people raised their hands.

"Bull!" I said to them. *"You are all fooling yourselves, and I'm going to prove it."* I then asked for a show of hands of those people who had seen a play in the last week or so.

No hands.

I then asked to see the hands of people who had seen a movie in the last week or so.

Many hands.

Bond, this phenomenon is common. All of us, including thee and me, have a slightly shrewd idea of ourselves. We often try to convince others and ourselves that we are something we are not, something we have an idea we "should" be.

Therefore, truth, my good son, can be determined NOT by how people use their mouths, but rather, how they use their wallets.

I want to burn this message into your mind. Be skeptical of what people say. Be skeptical of surveys. Of questionnaires. Instead, believe in numbers. For example, if everybody you talk with says they like plays more than movies, and yet the numbers say that 10,000 times more people buy movie tickets, then you believe the numbers!

If it looks like a duck, walks like a duck and quacks like a duck - guess what? It's probably a duck!

So keep reading the "SRDS" book. Keep looking at hot mail order publications and repeat mail order ads. Get yourself on as many mail order lists as possible. (Get a P.O. Box.) Watch the offers you receive. Anything you are going to buy anyway, and you can purchase by mail - do so.

Keep your finger on the pulse of the industry. Stay aware. Keep awake to the possibilities of overlooked marketing opportunities. After a while, you will develop a sixth sense.

Here's a true story that illustrates what I am trying to get across. It has long been my belief that a lot of money can be made by making offers to people who are at an emotional turning point in their lives. For example, when they have just had a baby, just gotten married, just lost a loved one, just gotten a raise, just filed bankruptcy, just purchased a new car, and so on.

Well, guess what? For a long time I have been wishing there was a way to get a list of pregnant women. Now there is! While looking through the "SRDS" I discovered that now you

STOP 11:35

START AGAIN
11:40

can rent 120,000 new names of pregnant mothers every month. Oh boy! Well, I got myself a hold of an M.D. who is very skilled in research in the areas of human and animal intelligence and I have commissioned him to write a report titled "How To Raise Your Child's IQ Before It Is Even Born!

This is exciting. Let's talk numbers. I plan to sell the report for $19.95 + $2.75 postage and handling. (Total $22.70) My fulfillment costs will probably be (including the 10% I pay the doctor) about $5.00. This means that every sale will yield a $15.00 contribution to overhead. Now, let's assume I'll get a 5% response. This means, of course that out of every 1,000 letters I mail, I will be receiving a total of 50 orders at $22.70, or a total gross income of $1,135.00. Now let's deduct $5.00 per order for fulfillment (which is $5.00 x 50 orders or $250) from this $1,135.00, and as you can see, we will have $885.00 left. Now, of course, we must also deduct the cost of the mailing. I figure it will cost (including list rental) about $400 per M (thousand) to mail a promotion like this. Thus, when we deduct this $400 from the $885.00 we have left to play with, you will see that we have a profit of $485.00 for every thousand letters mailed.

Hot damn! I'm cooking now! I'm glad I decided not to rest.

Onward. Let's see now $485.00 profit per M times 120M equals a
total profit of $58,200.

EVERY MONTH!

STOP 11:54

START AGAIN
12:23

P.S. I'm sitting here with Bobby B and I have just discovered how to
get Paul Harvey on my new radio. What I get is a very weak signal
from KABC but, my other co-worker Jack (The Plantation Nigger) (he's
really white) has just shuffled over. Jack told me earlier, that you
can get Paul also at 2:30. Maybe I'll interrupt my running and see
if I can get him then.

STOP 12:27

I LOVE YOU AND
GOOD LUCK!

Dad

UPDATE:

Kevin and I struggled with the decision, but ultimately, we decided to leave all the letters
unedited because it is a powerful reminder that Gary Halbert is writing this from prison
surrounded by all kinds of people.

For what it's worth, I never saw my father pass up a racist joke but I also never saw him treat
anyone differently based on race.

Onward...

The ability to recognize reality apart from what people say is key to really understanding your
prospects and how to turn them into customers.

After the initial copy dump where I pound out all my thoughts for a sales letter on a keyboard,
I re-read whatever I wrote and apply the "so what" test.

I once took a speech class in college and everyone had to give a speech on something they
are passionate about.

One of my fellow classmates was training to become a police officer and his speech was on
why he wanted to become a cop.

Everyone had to make three points and his were:

He got respect
He often got free food
He could get out of speeding tickets.

There wasn't a single mention of protecting or serving the public.

At first, I thought, "finally… a little honesty" but I quickly realized he may not be the sharpest person to give a badge and a gun.

I'm not saying police officers don't like to protect and serve, and I have never heard a full-fledged police officer say the best part of his job was power, free stuff and the ability to break the law.

But they can't hate those perks. Who would?

My point is simply that even the good men and women in law enforcement usually choose the politically correct answer over their feelings.

One big key to having marketing eyeglasses is to be honest with yourself.

Do you really enjoy getting up and going to the gym or do you really take pleasure in the sense of accomplishment or the afterglow?

The more honest you are with your true self and others, the faster you will see what really motivates people.

The Boron Letters
Chapter 9

Wednesday, 10:30 AM
June 20, 1984

Dear Bond,

Well, kiddo, I don't exactly know what I'm going to write about today so what I am going to do is just keep putting words down on paper until I start to get some direction.

It occurs to me that I need to tell you that just because I told you how to pick the very best lists doesn't mean that the less responsive lists are not valuable. Never forget the coat-of-arms promotion. That was mailed (and very successfully) to names taken from the white pages of the telephone book.

I guess what I want to start on today is how to think about developing a mail order campaign. And, as I said earlier, from now on, a good part of your working life should be spent reading the "SRDS" list book and newspapers and magazines that carry a lot of MO advertising.

Hey, by the way, I jogged the hill 4 times (non-stop) yesterday!

Well, anyway, I myself have recently been thumbing through the "SRDS" book and an interesting idea has occurred to me. There is, as you shall see when you start using the book, a big section devoted to compiled lists. All compiled lists are, by the way, names and addresses of people or businesses or institutions or whatever that have something in common.

For example: brick layers, architects, chiropractors, churches, businesses who do a $500,000 gross every year, business who do $1,000,000 every year, YMCA's, police stations, veteran purchasing agents, etc., etc.

O.K., here's my idea: What if you took the following headline:

**How You Can
Make Extra Money**

And, then you customize it to something like: "How Architects Can Make Extra Money" or "How Churches Can Make Extra Money" or "How Chiropractors Can Make Extra Money" etc., etc.

Now, let's say that we hire somebody to write a little report for us. The first part of the report tells about certain little-known techniques for making and investing money that anybody can use. The second part of the book would contain money-making techniques that would uniquely apply to a particular group of people, such as architects or chiropractors. (By the way, chiropractors are greedy so they would be one of my first targets!)

Anyhow, let's say our report is finished and so, now, we write a letter incorporating the idea that I previously expressed in those sample headlines. Perhaps the letter would start out like this:

```
Dr. Charles L. Davidson
1016 Ocean Ave.
Santa Monica, CA 90402

Dear Dr. Davidson,

   I am writing to you because I have discovered a great new
way for doctors of chiropractic to make a great deal of
extra money.

   It's really incredible and I am surprised no one has
thought of it before. Here's what it is all about: blah
blah, blah.
```

The letter would, of course, go on to describe the report and ask
him to buy a copy.

Now, let's suppose we sell the report for $20.00, and let us
further suppose that when we mail our letters, we find that we get a
very modest 4% response.

Now for the numbers. I'm going to stop here a moment and check the
"SRDS" and see how many bone snappers there are.

STOP 11:07 AM

START AGAIN
11:11 AM

That took 4 minutes. There are more than 33,000 chiropractors we
can mail to. Now, let's figure it will cost us $400 per thousand (M)
to mail out our letters. That's $400 per M x 33M, or a total mail
out cost of $13,200. Now at a 4% response we will get 1,320 orders.
Multiply 1,320 orders times $20.00 per order, and we will have total
sales of $26,400. When we subtract our mailing cost of $13,200 from
our sales revenue, we have left $13,200. Now we must also subtract
our cost of filling the orders. Since it shouldn't cost more than
$4.00 apiece on the outside, our total fulfillment cost will be
$4.00 per order times 1,320 orders, or $5,280.00. When we subtract
this figure from the $13,200 we have left, we will be left with a
net profit of $9,920.00.

Not a fortune but not to be sneezed at either. Especially when you consider that what I have described is less than 30 days work.

But, if this idea actually works, we have something much more valuable

STOP 11:21

START AGAIN
11:23

than our $9,920.00 profit. Yes indeed, my boy. You see, if this idea works what we have is a "winning formula"!

You see, my son, what we can do is keep the first section of our report the same and then customize the last half of the report (it will probably be more like the last 1/3) for different groups. Then, of course, the first line of our letter will talk about a great new way for plumbers to make extra money. Or architects. Or brick layers. Or preachers. Or dentists. Etc., etc.

Mucho bucks!

What'dya think of that? Right here before your eyes your old man has, during his lunch hour, come up with a brand new money maker!

No wonder they call me "The Legend."

More later.

STOP 11:29

START AGAIN
12:12

Seriously, what I have just described seems to me like a good idea and, more importantly, it helps a little to illustrate, as I said earlier, how to think about mail order!

It also illustrates the important concept of customization. As a general rule, the more "custom tailored" your promotion, is the more successful it will be.

For example, suppose you get a letter in the mail that says: "Dear Occupant, Here is news about a great new way to make money. Etc., etc., etc."

Mildly interesting. But now read this!

```
Dear Bond,


Here is a great new way for 16 year old kids to make money.
Blah, blah, blah, etc., etc., etc.
```

Quite a difference, right? Just imagine that you were to
receive such a letter on or right after June 26. It sure
would get your attention much more than the first letter,
wouldn't it?

And notice this: The second letter is not only customized
(as it is for 16-year-olds), it is also personalized because
it refers to you by name. The "Dear Bond" and the "16-year-
old kids" part of the letter really zeroes in on you,
doesn't it?

Here's another example of customization. Suppose you were writing
an ad about a book that tells how to buy real estate with no money
down. Your headline might look something like this:

How To Buy Real Estate
With No Money Down

Now let's boogie. Try this on for size!

How To Buy L.A. Real Estate
With No Money Down

Much better, eh? As a matter of fact, I <u>did</u> write an ad for such a
book and I <u>did</u> customize the ad and it <u>did</u> work much better.

Know this: Ideas breed other ideas.

For example, it just occurred to me that in addition to offering
chiropractors, plumbers, and so on a customized way to make money,
we could also offer them a customized way to buy real estate. And,
in this case, perhaps the first line in our letter might be: "Dear
Doctor X, Here's a unique way L.A. chiropractors can purchase
California real estate with no money down. Etc., etc."

UPDATE:

This technique is more powerful than ever because there is a trade off with great customization. Changing headlines for each paper used to cost extra money, which is no longer the case.

Also, your goal with customization is to customize the letter until the extra cost doesn't make up for the additional profits.

Nowadays, it is so cheap to segment and customize online promotions by interest, sex, age, location etc., and it's cheap to customize headlines and subject lines.

You can easily afford to set up a sales page with a headline like, "Where To Hide Your Gold Coins At Home!" for traffic from gold buyers and then set up another page with a headline, "Where To Hide Your Diamond Ring" for people who just bought rings.

Customization is so cheap, and most the other guys fail to use a lot of it, so this is an excellent way to lick the competition.

The Boron Letters
Chapter 10

Thursday, 9:12 a.m.
June 21, 1984

Dear Bond,

 Well, here I sit for the second day in a row starting my letter to you without knowing exactly what I am going to write about.

 B. tells me there seems to be some confusion over my gambling deal with *(name deleted)* in Las Vegas. This has me upset. I am trying to get *(name deleted)* on the telephone and clear up this matter. Unfortunately, though, it is clouding my mind at the moment.

 Yesterday, as you will recall, I just started writing and, lo and behold, something excellent came out. You know Bond, that fact contains a lesson in itself.

 And the lesson is that when you get stuck or emotionally jammed up one of the ways to get yourself unclogged and flowing again is just to keep moving. Run. Walk. Jog. Write. Do the dishes. Or whatever. But don't sit around waiting for a flash from Heaven.

 It doesn't work that way. Not often anyway. The key is <u>movement</u>!

 Let's see now. Hopefully I've got you doing road work, strengthening your muscles, fasting one day a week and eating well plus interfacing (isn't that a dandy buzzword?) with hot mail order publications and the "SRDS" list book.

 What's next? I know. Let's start teaching you how to actually create an ad or a good direct mail promotion. Here's how to get started. The first thing I'd like you to do is get a hold of two books. One is <u>Scientific Advertising</u> by Claude Hopkins and the other is <u>The Robert Collier Letter Book</u> by Robert Collier. Ask B. and Eric for help with getting these books. Read both of these books. Read <u>The Robert Collier Letter Book</u> two times and read <u>Scientific Advertising</u> three times. The first time you read these books, do so at your own pace. Don't take notes. Just read for enjoyment. However, after the first reading, I want you to take notes as you read the books the second and third times.

O.K., the next thing you need to do is get yourself a copy of my book that has "2001 Headlines" and read it. Then get Ben Suarez's book "SuperBiz" and read the headlines in his book. Keep going.

Make yourself a collection (a "swipe file") of good ads and good DM pieces and read them and take notes. (Eric and B. can help.)

Alright, now, after all this you should be ready to start the process. Let's concentrate on DM. Here's how to create a DM promotion from scratch:

Step 1 - Keep going through the "SRDS" book and looking at lists until you find one that you want to try to work.

Step 2 - Let's pretend you have chosen a list of people who have bought a book on how to make money in real estate. Now what you need to do is get three or four hot books in investing in real estate and read them and take notes.

Step 3 - OK now, you should get as many DM pieces and space ads on real estate investing you can find. Read these and take notes.

Step 4 - By now ideas will be churning around in your mind because you have fed your brain a lot of good stuff to work with. What you do at this point is go back and review your notes from "The Robert Collier Letter Book" and "Scientific Advertising" and read those headlines again.

Now, by now, I can almost guarantee that a central selling idea will have emerged from your cunning little mind.

Now, I don't know what that idea will be but let's say you have figured out how to personalize and customize your real estate investment offer as I discussed yesterday. And now, let's say your idea is to promise your potential customer that you are going to tell him how to buy real estate in <u>his area</u> with no money down. Then, your letter might start something like this:

```
Dear Mr. X,

Did you know that
there is now a way
to buy L.A. real
estate without
making any down
payment whatsoever?
Etc., etc., blah,
blah, blah.
```

Of course, that first sentence will be customized for every customer depending where he lives. Note: In this example I am assuming we are using computer letters. So, anyway, the letters would say

"to buy L.A. real estate"

Or

"to buy Detroit real estate"

Or

"to buy Key West real estate"

Etc., etc. Now, pay attention. Let's examine a way to "double customize" this offer. Let's say we have found a list of people in a specific occupation who like to invest such as cardiologists for example. Now, let's start our letter like this:

```
Dear Dr. X,

Did you know that
there is now a way
for a cardiologist
to buy L.A. real
estate without
making any down
payment whatsoever?
Etc., etc., blah,
blah, blah.
```

Bullseye! O.K. Now we've got the list picked out, we've got an idea for a product, we've got our central selling idea, and we are now ready for:

Step 5 - What you do at this point is create your product, and here is how you do it. First, you go back to those books on real estate investing and you extract in outline form all the good ideas in these books. Then, you pick out the best of the ideas and overlay them with the ideas you will have by now come up with yourself. Next, you arrange these ideas in some logical form and you start writing. Please remember, what we are creating here is a report <u>NOT</u> a book. I figure it should be something like 100 typewritten pages.

Now, please remember this: If you do this properly, you will have created something of considerable value. After all, what you will have done (hopefully) is taken a few good books on real estate investing, stripped away the garbage, and created a tight informative roadmap to real estate riches. Hey, how about that? Didn't I tell you that if you just keep flowing that something of value will emerge? Just look what has just slipped out of my mind! Did you catch it?

**The Amazing L.A. Roadmap
To Real Estate Riches!**

Not bad, eh? Now, we've got the title for our report!

More tomorrow.

STOP 10:12 AM

I LOVE YOU AND
GOOD LUCK!

Dad

UPDATE:

With eBooks and the explosion in self-publishing, it is much harder to stand out. This is where just a little work pays off big.

You see, the market is saturated with information products merely rephrasing what most of the industry leaders say but…

A little originality goes a long way in promoting your info products, and it is very easy to come by.

In fact, it's nearly impossible to go through any learning curve and not wish you had known something right from the start or discovered a slightly better way of doing something.

These original ideas become your unique solution or hook!

For example, I play around with a website just to use as a learning tool for myself and my daughter.

One day I pretended I was my own client looking to raise my click through rate.

I decided to toss in a picture, give the photo a title and make both the title and the pic a link.

This was back when most everyone said this would kill the click through rate, but I didn't care because this is a testing ground.

Thank god I didn't listen because the CTR went up 400% and I have been adding compelling pics to my emails ever since.

Just messing with the email system, I learned a lot of valuable things I think people should learn first.

I could write a valuable report titled "Email Marketing: What To Learn First And Who To Learn It From."

Now once your solution is unique, you spread the word quickly and publicly so you get credit for being an early adopter and…….

Until you are ripped off……you will enjoy a serious leg up on the competition.
You won't have to struggle for an answer to how your course is different from the others.

To peruse markets, I'd also suggest Clickbank, Amazon, and The New York Times Non-Fiction Best Sellers list, BUT ONLY PAY ATTENTION TO WHAT STAYS ON TOP WITHOUT BEING FREE!

There are a lot of $1 best sellers and people who climbed the ranks for a day or two by switching the book to free and then turning it back to charging.

These places will let you know what info markets are hot, and sometimes, you can see cross-over ideas others don't because they are married to one subject.

I'd also like to add that it is easier than ever to make money working with subjects you love because it is so much easier to target a lot of customers into very odd or strange things.

Look at it this way, if your true passion in life was only shared with 1% of the people you run into.

The USA alone has an estimated 315,000,000 people, and 1% would leave you 3.15 million potential customers.

And, let's suppose you are into something really whack and only 1 in 1,000 people would buy your product.

Now, let's pretend you are so vile and deviant, only 1 in 10,000 people feel the same desire.

That's still a potential pool of 31,500 people with the same crazy thinking you have. That's just in the USA.

In fact, I bet it will be hard to find competition is in such a highly-targeted and bizarre subject, which means it will be even easier for you to dominate that market, and finding those customers is easier than ever, so work with a subject you love.

The Boron Letters
Chapter 11

Friday, 9:07 AM
June 22, 1984

Dear Bond,

 As I left you yesterday, we had just came up with a working title
for our real estate investment report. I believe it was "The Amazing
L.A. Roadmap To Real Estate Riches!"

 Maybe we can come up with a better title but this one is fine. At
least for now. I believe we have also discussed extracting the
goodies from several real estate books, and we have collected and
examined other DM pieces and MO ads for books and so forth that deal
with real estate investments. We know how to choose a list to test,
and now it's time for us to create the DM promotion.

 The first thing we are going to discuss is the outside envelope.
This is where most mailers mess up first. You see, what most mailers
do is put so-called "teaser copy" on the outside envelope and, in
general, design the envelope so that it is very obvious that it
contains a sales pitch.

 If you will turn the page, I will show you what a typical direct
mail outer envelope looks like. Whoops. We're here already!

```
 ABC Publishing                      Bulk Rate 6666
 209 5th Ave.                    (bulk rate indicia
 New York, NY 10049             with permit number
  (Corner card with
  company Name)
                     John Jones
                  2193 7th Street
                  Akron, OH 10104
                  (Cheshire Label)
 WOW! There is exciting
 News inside.
 (Teaser Copy)
```

Pretty obvious, isn't it? In time, you are going to read my semi-famous A-Pile, B-Pile lecture. But here is a preview:

It is my contention that everybody divides their mail every day into two piles. An "A-Pile" and a "B-Pile". The "A" pile contains letters that appear to be personal. Like letters from friends, relatives, business associates, and so on.

On the other hand, the "B" pile contains those envelopes that, like the example above, obviously, contain a commercial message.

Now, here's the way it works: Everybody always opens <u>all</u> of their "A" pile mail. And for obvious reasons. After all, everybody wants to read their personal mail.

What happens to the "B" pile mail? Does it always get opened? No. It doesn't. Sometimes it is thrown away immediately without the envelope ever being opened. Sometimes, if it looks interesting, "B" pile envelopes will be set aside for later examination. And, of course, sometimes... **IF** the envelope looks interesting, or **IF** the person receiving it has some idle time, or **IF** the person is bored and has nothing else to do, than, **MAYBE** the "B" pile envelopes will be opened.

Unsatisfactory.

Quite obviously, people aren't getting to order from you unless they <u>read</u> your promotion and, also, quite obviously, they can't read your promotion unless they open the envelope.

And so, my dear son, what is our first objective here, as we begin to design our DM promotion? You are right! Our first objective is to get our envelope into the "A" pile.

And, it's so easy to do! All we have to do is make the envelope
look personal. (Or at least we will take pains so it doesn't look
commercial.) Here is what our envelope should look like:

```
┌─────────────────────────────────────────────────────┐
│ 209 - 5ᵗʰ Ave.              Live 20¢ Stamp           │
│ New York, NY 10049      (1ˢᵗ Class Stamp)            │
│ (corner card with                                    │
│ return address)                                      │
│                                                      │
│                  John Jones                          │
│                  2193 - 7th St.                      │
│                  Akron, OH  10104                    │
│               {a handwritten or typed                │
│                 address; no label}                   │
│                                                      │
└─────────────────────────────────────────────────────┘
```

Nearly everybody who receives this envelope will open it. Why? The answer, as a copywriter would say, is simple. A person who gets this envelope will open it to find out what is inside.

Because it is intriguing.

Because it looks personal.

Because it might be from someone he knows.

Because it does not <u>OBVIOUSLY</u> contain a personal message.

Yes, my dear son, for all these good reasons, the person who gets this envelope will open it in order to find out what is inside.

You see, the "B" pile envelope lets the recipient know right from the jump that it contains a commercial message. And, of course, the recipient <u>ALREADY KNOWS</u> that this envelope does not contain any sort of personal communication.

Too bad. Too bad for the mailer, that is. Because, and this should be painfully apparent, because if only half as many people open your envelope, only half as many even have a CHANCE to order!

So obvious, so simple and so <u>OVERLOOKED</u>!

Yes, it's true. As obvious as this should be, it is missed by almost every advertising agency and nearly every so-called "direct mail expert" in the country.

So, I'll get off my podium. If I haven't made my point by now, shame on me. And, now, let's assume that we have designed an "A" pile envelope and we are relatively sure that our envelope will be opened. What's next? What's next is that we must now get our potential customer to <u>begin</u> reading our sales letter.

How do we do that? Well, let's start by getting his attention. And intriguing the heck out of him right from the start. Let's try this: Let's get a little plastic baggie and put some dirt in it and then attach it to the top of our letter. Here is what the letter will look like:

{little zip lock baggie
attached here with
dirt inside}

Friday, 6:30 p.m.

June 12, 1984
{typed day and date and time}
Dear Mr. Jones,
{personal salutation}

~~~~~~
{body copy}
~~~~~~
{body copy}
~~~~~~
{body copy}
                                        (over)

                                        {little directive that
                                        tells the reader what
                                               to do from here}

Pay attention: What I have just shown you contains several of my little-known DM secrets. Let's examine them one by one.

First of all, that little baggie filled with dirt just sort of reaches right out and grabs you, doesn't it?

If you received this letter, wouldn't you be wondering, *"What's in this baggie?" "Is that dirt in there?" "Why would somebody be sending me a baggie of dirt?"*

And, consciously or unconsciously, you would be thinking, *"I better read this and find out what it is all about."*

And, you see, we now have not only captured our reader's attention, we have gotten his "focused" attention.

Quality attention.

Now, what about that part right above the salutation? The part that contains the day, date and time. What is the significance of all this? Tune in tomorrow and see!

I LOVE YOU AND GOOD LUCK!

Dad

Yesterday I ran (jogged) the hill 5 times non-stop in 58 minutes and 18 seconds and after the run I weighed 176-1/2 pounds.

UPDATE:

I have taken this lesson and translated it to emails, and if you pay close attention, you can smoke your competition when it comes to open rates.

Instead of physically sorting your email, you now sort your emails by using different email addresses.

Your primary or A-pile email address are your work and personal email addresses you must look at daily.

Then, if you are like most humans, you have a special address just for giving those pesky marketers who promise they have the solution to your problem and you can get more info by giving them your email address.

Now here is the kicker.

You sign up for a website using your spam or B-pile email address and then you must go into that account to click a link confirming your opt-in.

Once there you see you have 500 unopened messages and you either ignore them or delete them.

BUT!

When you go check your personal and work email accounts you see your spam box has a few emails in it so you open it and begin to scan the names and subjectlines to make sure nothing you really wanted slipped through the cracks.

This means…

**It's Better To Be In
The Spam Box of A Primary Email Address Than
To Be In The Primary Box of A Spam Email Address!**

Worry about getting a good address before worrying about deliverability and what words will get you labeled as spam.

I usually get double the industry standard open rates and a lot goes into getting 50% and higher open rates but it all starts before prospects enter an email address.

You still need great subject lines and a lot goes into what the list is trained to expect.

If you want to learn more about this end of what I do, visit bondhalbert.com

Saturday, 10:02 AM
June 23, 1984

Dear Bond,

Let's get right back to that real estate letter. I've already pointed out how that little baggie filled with dirt will attract and focus our reader's attention. Now, let's talk about the other particulars of the first page of that letter.

I think I left off in my last letter where I was just about to comment on the part above the salutation, the part that tells the day of the week, the exact time, the day of the month, and the year. Why is it important to put these specifics in the letter?

Well, it makes the letter a little more personal, doesn't it? I mean seriously, don't you feel a little closer to me because I put all this data in each of my letters to you? I think so. I think this way of doing things bonds the writer and the reader closer together. It also gives our transmission the quality of immediacy. And, while I'm on the subject, it just occurred to me that I should tell you that another additional way to achieve this bond of intimacy and immediacy in your letters is to describe where you are and what you are doing as you are writing the letter.

For example, right now I am sitting cross-legged on my back here in room 7 of dorm 6 in the Boron Federal Prison Camp. I have just finished running the hill five times (4 miles), and I did it in 57 minutes and 5 seconds.

Do you see how this type of personal, _specific_ info bonds the reader and writer closer together? You do? Good. I'll continue.

Now, here's another little thought: When you tell the day of the week plus the exact time you are writing the letter, it makes it seem a more important communication too, doesn't it? Sort of like a telegram. There's no doubt about it: A time-dated communication carries considerable more weight than one which is not.

Onward.

Now let's talk about the salutation. Notice that the salutation addresses our reader by name, just like I do in these letters to you. "Dear Bond" gets a certain quality of focused attention that is not enjoyed by "Dear Sir" or "Dear Occupant" or "Dear Reader".

Think about it. When you read the words "Dear Bond", you know my letter is for you personally, don't you? It's not for Kevin. It's not for whoever owns the house. Or anybody who lives at the address on the envelope. No. The words "Dear Bond" indicate that this letter is for you and you alone.

And this makes you pay more attention, doesn't it?

Now, if you will look in the lower right hand corner of the letter in my illustration and, also, in all of my other letters, you will see, in parenthesis, a tiny little instruction like this: **(over)** or like this: **(go to page 7)**. What I am doing here is taking the reader by the hand and leading him exactly where I want him to go. It seems like a small point and, maybe it is, but is the little touches like this that keeps the letter flowing, the reader moving along, and, it relieves him of the burden of trying to figure out what he is supposed to do when he finishes reading a particular page.

Don't scoff. Quite often (most often) your letter will arrive when your prospect is busy, when his mind is on other things. Therefore, you need to work hard to make reading your letter pleasant, easy-read, interesting, and unconfusing.

                                                    STOP 10:39

START AGAIN
6:38

Well, here I am once again starting to write without knowing where I am going. All I know is that when I keep moving and writing and flowing, generally something decent emerges. We'll see.

No, wait. I know what I'll tell you. How about what else goes inside the carrier envelope in addition to the letter? One thing for sure is that you must include a reply envelope. Now, when it comes to reply envelopes, you basically have two choices. The options are to make the reader pay the postage when he mails the envelope, or for you to pay the postage for him. There are two ways for you to pay the postage. One of these is to simply put a "live" stamp on the envelope so that it will be all ready to mail when he receives it.

There are a couple of advantages to this strategy and one big disadvantage. The disadvantage is cost. Right now, at 20¢ per stamp it will cost you $200.00 extra per thousand to do business this way. And, naturally, because of this, most mailers never even test this option.

That's too bad. Really. Because sometimes, this strategy will pay off. Therefore, I believe, when either or both of the following conditions exists, you should test a SRE (Stamped Reply Envelope):

Condition #1: You are selling a high-ticket item where the profit structure is such that one additional sale per thousand letters mailed will yield more than enough profit to pay for your SRE's.

This means, of course, that each sale you make has to have a mark up of at least $200.00.

You know what? What I just wrote may not be quite accurate. Because, if you think about it, if those SRE's bring in two or more orders per M, then your mark up on each sale would only have to be $100.00. If they bring in three extra orders per M, the mark up would only have to be $70.00 per unit to make it feasible.

And so on.

Condition #2: You should test a SRE whenever you can make the recipient of your letter feel guilty if he doesn't reply. This works especially well for charity or fund raising letters. For example, you might have a line in one of your letters that goes something like this:

"...and those pitiful children need your help right now! So please send a check immediately and send as much as possible. That's all you have to do. I have already addressed the reply envelope and I have even gone to the expense of putting a stamp on it so you won't have to hunt for one!"

Pretty good guilt, eh? And you can also use guilt in a regular sales letter. Here's how:

Continued Tomorrow

I love you and
Good Luck!

Dad

UPDATE:

This lesson is very much overlooked by many of today's online marketers but not the guys at the top.

Just using a 3d looking buy button makes a small difference in sales and reducing the number of steps required to order adds a lot.

One key question every business owner should ask is "how can I make it so ordering is even easier."

Many great burger stands went out of business when the competition across the street added a drive thru.

The Boron Letters
Chapter 13

Sunday, 9:02 AM
June 24, 1984

Dear Bond,

Well, I've found myself a little hideaway near the top of "The Hill" and I am sitting cross-legged (yoga style) on a blanket. I am looking out over good old Camp Boron and writing you this letter.

Did you pay attention to yesterday's lessons? Have you noticed how I have already used, in this letter, many of the little ideas I talked about yesterday?

You did notice? Good. Then I guess it's safe to go on.

But before I do (there's a baby rabbit about 7 yards from me!), I want to tell you that I just talked to your mom and it put some pain in my brain. She works hard, and now that I am in here, she more or less feels she's out there all alone against the wolves. Rick wants money. Chuck wants money. Your mom has bills and I feel very pressured.

It hurts.

But you once said the smartest thing I've ever heard a kid say. You said that you were luckier than Jeff because when Jeff lived with me, I was already rich, and that you get to be with me when I am not rich and, therefore, you get to learn how I solve problems, especially money problems.

Well, maybe we can both learn something today. (NOTE: I say "well" almost as often as Ronnie Reagan, don't I?) What I feel like doing is sniveling. I'd love to take some drugs or alcohol and forget my problems. Or maybe just lie on my bunk all day and read a book.

At the very least I'd like to eat. But I can't. I can't because this is my day to fast. And to write to you. And to Z. And to work on a new ad for L. Etc.

And, so I shall. Not because (that bunny is still right here!) I want to but, rather, because I need to. You see, when things are tough I have discovered that a very very simple (but effective) thing to do is just keep moving in some sort of positive direction.

And... and... let's talk about envelopes and little baggies filled with dirt. O.K. as I recall, I was just about to tell you how to use a SRE to induce guilt in a regular commercial DM sales pitch.

Here's how: What you do is write something like this:

> *...and so, Mr. Jones, as you can see, what I am*
>
> *offering you is a once-in-a-lifetime opportunity to own*
>
> *a piece of a legalized Nevada whorehouse. I hope you*
>
> *can take advantage of this offer. But, if you can't,*
>
> *would you please drop me a note and tell you can't*
>
> *participate at this time. That way I'll feel free to*
>
> *make this exciting offer to someone else. I've enclosed*
>
> *a self-addressed envelope and I have even put a stamp*
>
> *on it because (either way) it is important that I hear*
>
> *from you right away.*
>
> *Please, please -- reply **today**!*

Many lessons in that little block of copy. First of all, it's not just a guilt inducer, it also develops a strong selling point: Namely, the selling point of this being a genuine limited offer that some other lucky person will take advantage of it you don't. And, the stamped envelope tends to "credential" that point. (I just made a noise and my little bunny slipped away.) Here's something else: If you can get a person who is <u>not</u> going to order to agree, in his mind, to write and tell you he is not going to, then you will get more orders.

Can you guess why? Aha, you didn't get this one, did you, smart alec? No matter. I'll tell you why. You see, what happens sometimes is that a person who is getting a pen or pencil and a piece of paper in order to write you and tell you "No" will sometimes start thinking like this: *"Well, you jerk. I'd kind of like to get in on this deal anyway and now that I've got the pen and paper I may as well go ahead and order."*

Now, let's switch our discussion to another kind of envelope where you also pay the postage for your customer. I'm talking about, of course, the good old standby known as a BRE or "Business Reply Envelope".

You've seen thousands of BRE's. They look like this:

```
                                                    Bulk Rate
                                                    Permit #6666

            If Mailed In U.S. Postage Will Be Paid By

                 Nevada Inc.
                 201 Anywhere Road
                 Las Vegas, NV   20215
```

Most mailers love BRE's. They have the advantage of making it easy
for the customer to reply plus the advantage of being much cheaper
than a stamped reply envelope.

The reason they are cheaper is that you only pay the postage (and
BRE fee) for those envelopes that are actually mailed back to you.

However, they also have some disadvantages. Like these:

1.   They slow up your mail. The post office has to tabulate
how many BRE's you get each day so they'll know how much you
owe. This will hold up your mail (<u>and your cash flow</u>!) for <u>at
least</u> one extra day. Maybe more.

2.   They telegraph that yours is not, in fact, a real personal
letter. You know, sooner or later, you've got to let your
potential customers know that you want him to buy something.
However, if you let him know <u>immediately</u> quite often he won't
even give you a hearing. And, in truth, this is a disservice to
him. Because, quite often, after he reads your info he will
discover that what you have to offer has genuine value to him.
So try to strategize your mailings so that he at least reads
your letter <u>before</u> he makes a decision.

3.   You can't do good guilt with a BRE. SRE's are much better
for this purpose.

And now, let's talk about yet another type of reply envelope. I call it the PSH envelope. PSH stands for "Place Stamp Here". They look like this:

```
                                                            Place
                                                            Stamp
                                                            Here


         If Mailed In U.S. Postage Will Be Paid By

         Nevada Inc.
         201 Anywhere Road
         Las Vegas, NV  20215




```

This is the most economical reply envelope of all. That's because (obviously) the customer pays the postage. Let's talk about this envelope: First of all, it's not as convenient for the customer so you will <u>lose</u> some orders because of that. On the other hand, this envelope is more personal so you will <u>gain</u> some orders because of that.

(Guess what, Bondy? I think a solution to your mom's money problems just popped into my mind!)

Now, of course, this envelope isn't as personal as an SRE but it is more than a regular BRE. It is, as I have pointed out, cheaper than both.

What it is, then, is cheaper than a SRE and more personal than a BRE and, in my judgment, this is the best envelope for most mailers to use.

More mailers should test PSH envelopes and carefully analyze the results. Many of them are going to be surprised.

DAMN! I'm getting a little tired of writing about envelopes. I think I'll switch over to discussing that little baggie filled with dirt.

However, my hour is up and I've got to go stand count. (They want to know where I am all the time. They must like me!)

Tune in again tomorrow.

UPDATE:

The first point my father makes in the letter is to keep on keeping on. Here is a trick to doing so.

Keep two task lists.

The first list is of every important thing you really should do while at your best.

My distraction-free creative time is in the morning when I do most of my writing, editing or consulting, because it's when I am reliably at my best.

The second list is of all the important tasks which I can do equally well regardless of my mood.

Whenever I get stuck in the morning or feel off, I simply take care of some of the important business which quickly puts me back into an uplifting and productive mood.

Another trick my father taught me was to work in libraries because we are social animals and it is really hard to be in the library and not try and work. Especially inside the research section but nowadays you can get a similar affect from coffee houses where all the hipsters congregate with their moleskin notebooks and mobile office in a backpack.

The marketing lesson about please reply works very well today.

Charities now send letters with several pre-paid envelopes.

The Boron Letters
Chapter 14

Monday, 9:05 AM
June 25, 1984

Dear Bond,

  Today we are going to talk about that baggie full of dirt that we have attached to our real estate investment sales letter.

  Now, listen up. While it is true that you must attract attention to your advertisements and sales letters, it is also true that your "attention grabber" should be relevant. It should tie in with your message. It should make sense.

  Once upon a time there was a guy who wrote a series of articles for a magazine called "Printers Ink." I forget the guys pen name but he was very good. He wrote about how to improve DM & MO advertising.

  Well, anyway, he once called an excellent example of how you should NOT attract attention. Check out this headline:

A Submarine That Flies?	
~~	~~~~~~~~~
~~	~~~~~~~~~
~~	~~~~~~~~~
~~	~~~~~~~~~
~~	~~~~~~~~~
~~	~~~~~~~~~

And then, beneath that headline was the copy: "No, we don't have a submarine that flies but our pink pills, etc., etc."

A cheap shot. People resent this kind of fraud. Don't do it. If you put your mind to work you won't have to either. You can grab attention without "cheating," without making the reader feel ripped off. Which brings me right back to our dirt-filled baggie.

Do you remember how I explained that the baggie has our reader wondering why you sent it to him? That he wants to know what's going on here? That we have his focused attention? Quality attention?

You say you do remember all that? Good. In that case, I'll proceed.

Now, here's how the letter will start off:

Dear Mr. Tiberion,

I am attaching a plastic baggie to the top of this letter for two important reasons:

First of all, what I have to say to you is very serious and I needed some way to be sure to get your attention.

And secondly, what is inside that baggie could very well be your passport to complete financial independence!

Why is this? The answer is simple: You see, what is inside that baggie is a very tiny amount of what is the most valuable thing on earth.

I'm talking about real estate and, in this case, *Hawaiian Real Estate!*

Yes, it's true. The sand inside that baggie was taken directly from a certain beach on the island of Maui and this particular beach is one of the few left that is open for purchase to private investors!

Here's what it's all about: blah, blah, blah, etc., etc., etc.

O.K., Bondodog, do you follow what I'm doing here? You see, what I did is I got his attention and then I tied my copy to my "attention grabber" in a relevant way that makes sense.

Now, if I were to continue writing this letter, I would use words that would make my reader "picture with pleasure" that beach in his mind. Before I was finished, he would be able to feel the sand in his toes, smell the fresh tang of the salt air, drink in the stars with his eyes and feel the warm friendly sun on his back.

Oddly enough, just a couple days ago, I received from Eric a copy of a sales letter he is writing to sell Hawaiian real estate. I am going to send Eric's letter to you real soon and I want you to read it. Then imagine how much his letter could be improved by using all the little secrets (including the baggie) that we have just discussed.

Well oh well, what have we got so far? Let's see: we picked out our list, we know how to think about outside envelopes and return envelopes, we have thought up a way to get our reader's attention, and we have the first couple paragraphs of our letter.

But, in most cases, we need more than a letter and a reply envelope. Yes, in most cases, it is good to include an order card and some type of printed brochure. I like to include an order card and a brochure with my sales letters. However, I do not like to let my reader see my order card, etc. as soon as he opens the envelope.

Do you know why? That's right. I don't want him to realize that I want to sell him something until I am well into my pitch. Here is something else you should know: Many people, when they read an ad, read it like this... What they do is, they read the headline first and then they go right to the order coupon.

The same is true with direct mail letters. If your reader sees your order card as soon as he opens your envelope, he will read it first to see what the deal is.

And, that's not good for us. It is true, of course, that we do want him to read our order card but we want him to read it at the proper time! And the proper time is after he has read our letter.

Comprende?

Now, how in the world do we include an order card and/or a sales brochure in our envelope and still hide it (temporarily) from our reader?

Believe it or not, it took me years to figure this out. And, just like the paperclip, it is so simple, you wonder why you didn't see it instantly.

Here's how I do it: What I do is, take an 8-1/2x11 piece of paper and cut it in half long ways.

```
(cut here)
 -  -   -   -   -
```

Next I fold the cut pieces in thirds like this:

```
(fold here)
 -   -   -

(fold here)
 -   -   -
```

Now, turn the piece around and write this on the back:

NOTE: Open this paper to find the special info mentioned in my letter.

GH

OK, now, that which I have just written should be printed in blue ink and appear to be handwritten. Notice that it refers him to my letter and it is personalized with my initials.

Now here is what he will see when he finally opens that note:

```
┌─────────────────────────────────┐
│ Here Is The Info I Mentioned    │
│      In My Letter!              │
│                                 │
│                  (Boxed         │
│                   Photo         │
│                   Here)         │
│                                 │
│                                 │
│                                 │
│   (Order Coupon)               │
│                                 │
│                                 │
│                                 │
└─────────────────────────────────┘
```

O.K., kiddo, here is my final point for the day. Although I like my letters to be personal, in most cases, I also like them to be "businesslike personal".

And, that's why part of the package should be typeset and maybe contain some photographs. Your see, this adds an air of stability to your promotion. It makes you seem like a real business.

Again, I want to emphasize that in order to make it easy to order (and to credential our offer) we need stuff like order cards, brochures, photos, and typeset copy.

But, again, as I said, we want our reader to see this stuff at the proper time.

AFTER HE HAS READ OUR LETTER!

I love you and
GOOD LUCK!

Dad

STOP 10:07

UPDATE:

Wow, this letter is loaded with marketing gold and a lot of it needs updated applications so here we go…

In your attempts to stand out, try and fight any urge to sound like a cliché and use phrases which a reader could finish on their own.

You only want the reader or viewer to get that head-nodding "been there, done that" feeling when you already got the prospect's attention.

There are many ways to do this, but one simple trick anyone can use is replace the adjectives in their headlines and opening statements with words from a CURRENT power list.

Marketing greats like my father and other top copywriters usually keep a power word list. Those power words begin to seep into their conversations as well as their copy. But you don't want to just use their lists.

Just like diets, words come in and out of fashion.

Consider these words: Keen, Cool, Funky, Hip, Hot, and Epic. You can almost tell the age of the people who use them.

Yes, you can tailor your words to your readers average age but you want to do that during the bonding part of the copy/script.

The main point is the power of individual words ebbs and flows.

Nobody is going to buy a book on a keen new way to pick up girls.

Cool new way would be pretty boring too.

Funky might stand out more, whereas in the 1980's, it was like keen is today.

Go look at tabloids and make a list of the words in headlines that really suck you in.

For instance, I like "crisis," which is a great replacement for problem.

Divide your list of words into positive and negative.

Now peruse the list right before you begin the copy dump when you write the majority of your copy in one sitting.

By the way, you can do 40 edits, but you want to write from start to finish in one sitting so your different moods on different days don't seep into your copy and make it disjointed.

Anyway, when you are finished with the copy dump, look for adjectives and things you can punch up on your list without sounding like a clown.

Another tip, when my dad says he uses picture words, he really means phrases and terms which paint a picture like cherry red.

Describe what it looks like when happy customers receive the benefit of your product.

For example, phrases like, "My clients wake up all excited and can't wait for the morning because............ they love to sip coffee while opening their email to see how much money they made while sleeping."

If this was a first person story, I'd add parts about looking out the window as the neighbors left for work while I take a shower.

Enough about pictures, let's update on avoiding the whole Oh Yuck factor.

This is really easy because what makes you say oh yuck also makes others say it.

Excessively talking about yourself, overly busy webpages, unexpected auto-playing videos and so forth give most everybody that oh yuck feeling but…

The main point is to disguise your pitch until you want the prospect to know you are selling something, and you can do this online to great effect.

Readers of snail mail do the same thing with websites and emails... they scroll right to the bottom.

Most marketers add a buy button to the bottom of their page, but instead of saying BUY, you might want to try adding my father's text or simply use the word "Next."

Now when they scroll down and back up again, the length of the copy and WILL affect their decision to read.

If you are online, add a few videos. They probably won't watch, but it makes the reader feel like they can just pick and choose what they are interested in reading.

You can also do this by using monster titles to let the copy appear to be broken up in sections but make those titles blind benefits.

Why Our Customers Are So Happy
blah blah blah

21 Uses For XYZ Product
blah blah blah

Life-Changing Results
blah blah blah

In print, these headings would tip the reader off to this being a sales message too soon but online….they look very normal.

Also, I'd like to add that the proper time to let people know you are pitching is after you have started seriously fueling their desire.

Tuesday, 9:09 AM
June 26, 1984

Dear Bond,

Happy Birthday!

You know son, you are the joy of my life. I hope you pass your driver's test today. But, if you don't, it's ok, just keep working on it untill you do.

Yesterday, as you remember, we left off after discussing the baggie and today, I think I need to begin to teach you the particulars of how to write copy.

As you will note, we haven't talked about writing copy as of yet. What we <u>have</u> talked about mainly is the "conceptualization" of our marketing effort. However, now that we have conceptualized our piles, let's get a little more technical about the whole process of writing copy.

Here's how to begin: The first thing you need to do is to assemble a file that contains everything you can get your hands on that is relevant to your promotion. Here are some of the things that might be included in your file:

1) List cards describing the lists you are going to test

2) A copy of the report you intend to sell

3) Copies of DM pieces that other people have used to sell products or services related to what you want to sell.

4) Copies of space ads that other people have used to sell products or services related to what you want to sell.

5) Copies of books and reports on real estate investing.

6) Copies of exceptionally good ads and DM pieces, even if they are not related to real estate.

7) A copy of that book I'm going to give you that contains hundreds of headlines.

8) Anything else you can think of that might be an "idea generator."

OK now, after you have assembled all this stuff, what you need to do is start reading and taking notes.

Now, here is a little quirk of mine: I have a special way of taking these notes which, incidentally, I call "nugget notes."

You see, what I do is take my notes in the form of little nuggets of information. When I am done the paper I have been writing on looks like this:

~~	~~~~~~~	~~~~~~~
~~	~~~~~~~~~	~~~~~~~~~
~~	~~~~~~~~	~~~~~~~~
~~	~~~~~~~	~~~~~~~
~~	~~~~~~~~~	~~~~~~~~~
~~	~~~~~~~~	~~~~~~~~
~~	~~~~~~~	~~~~~~~
~~	~~~~~~~~~	~~~~~~~~~
~~	~~~~~~~~	~~~~~~~~

Remember this when you are taking these notes don't stuff yourself.

Sometimes, my nugget notes consist of just one word. Sometimes they consist of meaningless phrases. Many times my notes make sense but many times they don't. No matter. I never worry about it. I just keep writing. I write what occurs to me as I read the list cards, the jackets of books, the ads, the DM pieces, and all the rest of the material I have assembled.

Now here are a few things you should always include. A complete description of your product including how many pages, how many words, how many photos, who wrote it, facts about the author (his age, background, success stories, etc.). You should also take notes on what this product will do for you. Will it make you wealthy? How will more money help your customer? Will he be able to buy a better car? Take more vacations? Afford a better home? If so, put it down.

OK now, after you have taken all these notes

what I want you to do is re-read the notes and the really good ones, put a star * beside them. And the ones that are even better put two stars ** next to them. And then, the red hot ones you put three *** or more stars beside them.

 Now, at this point, what you need to do is <u>stop</u> working on this project. That's right. Just let it go. Put it right out of your mind. Just go on about your other business for a day or two.

 Now then, often what happens during this time, is that an <u>outstanding</u> sales idea will occur to you. Sometimes this idea will be how to get attention, like with my baggie idea.

[Bond, I got interrupted here. Two prison guards came over and searched me and B. and told us to stay out of the little park where we take our breaks. Apparently, some little kid was caught smoking pot here yesterday.]

Ah well, that's life in the big city.

 So let's get started again. As I was saying, sometimes your breakthrough idea or "aha experience" will be a way to get attention like my baggie idea, or a new way to help the prospect visualize the benefits of owning what you have to sell, or a new order generating sales point or whatever. Anyway, at this point you now need to begin writing your letter according to formula.

 By formula, I mean you should work within a proven sequential outline like AIDA.

What does AIDA stand for? It stands for ATTENTION, INTEREST, DESIRE, ACTION. So, to make it clearer your letter should:

1. First, get his attention

2. Second, get him interested

3. Third, make him desire what you are selling

4. Compel him to take whatever action is needed to get whatever it is you are selling.

Tomorrow, we'll go over this in more detail. But for today, once again I want to wish you HAPPY BIRTHDAY!

I Love You And
Good Luck!

Dad

Whoops, I forgot to mark down the time but we'll make it 10:59

UPDATE:

This was by far the most pivotal birthday and changed my life forever in ways both good and bad but… this isn't about me.

I do however want to say that these Boron Letters were the single best gift anyone ever given me but I must confess…

I didn't know it at the time.

You see, my father mentions the time I told him I felt lucky to see how he makes money. Well, this took place when I was about 9 and from then on I was his protégé.

So I had been receiving these lessons by word of mouth for years but having them written is so much better because…

I can go over them often as many people do once a year.

They also serve as proof of an extraordinary childhood.

It's not easy to convince people you spent 20 years studying marketing when you are only 30 years old.

In fact I began lying and down playing previous experience just to make the truth sound more believable.

Okay, enough about me.

Keeping your whole project in a box really helps. My father kept a red wooden fodder box which sits next to my desk now and is among my favorite possessions.

Wait, I said enough about me. Sorry, won't happen again.

Now I want to add a few things about nugget notes. Keep a pen and paper with you at all times.

Brainstorms come at the times when your brain is well nourished and the most relaxed, which means the ideas come when you least expect them.

Some copywriters write on the computer and others, like my brother, are still inkers who use a pen and paper, but ALL great copywriters write their nugget notes, bullets, and headlines by hand.

You will lose ideas trying to remember how to record a note on your phone. One idea quickly rolls into another, so keep a pen and paper nearby at all times.

Also, rank everything in terms of what the buyer cares about. Unless your charity work is more proof of your expertise, it gets the lowest rank.

Remember, the copy is only about you in so much as it proves how you can help the prospect solve their problems.

The Boron Letters
Chapter 16

Wednesday, 9:09 AM
June 27, 1984

Dear Bond,

AIDA. As I said yesterday, it stands for attention, interest, desire, and action.

Now, let's talk about each of these four formula elements and how we will use them in our sales letter.

Attention comes first. Naturally, we must get our readers attention before he can become interested in and desirous of our offer. Getting attention is CRUCIAL. If you don't get it, your letter or advertisement will never be read. That's why I like to attach things to the top of my DM letters. I have attached coins, dollar bills, 2-dollar bills, Japanese "pennies", Mexican pesos etc. and there gimmicks has always gotten a lot of attention.

However, as I told you before, you must get the right kind of attention. If not, your reader will be insulted and angry and probably won't become a customer. So, always remember that your attention grabber needs to be relevant. It needs to tie in naturally with your letter.

Now, as we have discussed, we have decided to attach a plastic baggie filled with sand to the letter we are going to use to sell our report on real estate investing.

There's no doubt that this technique will get our reader's attention. It will really make him sit up and take notice. It will be the right kind of attention too. Because it is relevant. It has a natural tie in with the story our letter has to tell. Actually, we have, as you will recall, more or less written this part of the letter in an earlier lesson.

OK now, we have got attention, and our first few paragraphs have made a natural tie in with our "attention grabber." So, what's next? Well, referring right back to our AIDA formula we see that the next thing we need to do (after getting his attention) is catch his interest.

How do we do this? Well, let's start by feeding him interesting facts. Like how much money there is to be made by investing in Maui real estate. By telling how much sand (cubic tons) is on the beach where we got the sand in that baggie. By telling how this is one of the best beach front investment opportunities in Maui. By telling how many pretty girls there are around. By telling the specific kinds of fish you can catch right off the beach. Etc.

 OK, now after we have told him a lot of interesting facts our AIDA formula now tells us we should now arouse his desire.

 Here's how we do that.

STOP
9:43

START AGAIN
10:30

 Well, Bondo Dog, things get curiouser and curiouser. I just got fired from my job. I'll tell you the story when you visit; there's really not much to say and it's kind of boring so let's get back to our letter.

 So, meanwhile, back at the ranch, I believe we were talking about how to create desire, and as I was saying, here's how we do that: What we do to create desire is we describe the <u>benefits</u> our prospect gets if he buys our product or service. Now, in the case of an investment-orientated offer, what we have to offer is the prospect of making money. At least this is our <u>main</u> attraction. So, what's let's do is let's help him to picture in his mind the benefits of having more money. Don't think it's not necessary. Remember, <u>you must always do even the obvious</u>. Here then, are some benefits of having more money:

    <u>New car</u> - impress your friends and family, ride in comfort and luxury

    <u>Nice house</u> - comfort, luxury, and status

    <u>Peace of mind</u> - no worries about bills or financial emergencies

    <u>Vacations</u> - money lets you travel the world, go where you want when you want

STOP
10:42

START AGAIN
10:47

<u>Attract the opposite sex</u> - money, as any fool knows, makes you much more attractive to the opposite sex - it gives you more opportunities to meet them in nice places also

<u>Leisure time</u> - money buys time: perhaps the best reason of all for having fun goes

Alright kiddo, we've got his attention, we've got him interested, created desire and now what's left? Go back to our AIDA formula and you will see that that last "A" stands for action. And that's just what we've got to get, <u>action</u>! Action in the form of him sending us an order.

You should pay very close attention to how <u>I</u> get action in my MD and DM pitches. I do this better than anybody. I am very thorough when it comes to closing a sale. Here's a little of example of how I do it. "Would you like to get in on this great investment opportunity? Would you like to be one of the privileged few who actually own a piece of the finest beach in Maui? If so, it's easy to order. All you have to do is fill out the order coupon and send it to me with your payment, etc., etc."

One thing I want to stress is that you must be very clear, very specific about what you want him to do. Lead him by the hand and take him exactly where you want him to go. Tell him where the order coupon is. Tell him to fill it out. Tell him to enclose the payment. Tell him how much to send. Tell him who the checks and money orders should be made out to. Tell him to use the envelope. Tell him the envelope doesn't need a stamp. (If it doesn't.) Tell him to put the envelope in the mail.

And, above all, tell him to do all this <u>RIGHT NOW</u>! <u>TODAY</u>!

Tell him what he will get if he hurries and tell him what he will lose if he delays.

STOP
11:01

START AGAIN
11:02

Seriously, Bond, you should read my ads and DM pieces and pay particular attention to how I close the sales. Sometimes I devote as much as 25% or more of the entire ad to closing.

This, of course, has been just a few "starter ideas" on how to create a DM promotion. As I keep saying, I'm just warming up and will get more detailed later.

In the next couple days or so, I intend to send you Eric's sales letter and I want you to read it. Then see if you can see how everything I taught you in the last few days would make his letter more effective.

But, in the meantime, I have an assignment for you. Here's what I want you to do: what I want you to do is get a copy of the facelift ad and then sit down and copy it in your own handwriting. I want you to write it out just the way you would if you were going to take it to a secretarial service to have it typed. By the way, check with B on this and he'll tell you what format your hand written copy should be in.

And guess what? After you have completed this assignment I will explain why I am having you do this and how it will help you.

I LOVE YOU AND
GOOD LUCK!

Dad

STOP 11:11

P.S. I heard you got your driver's license! I'm very proud of you!

UPDATE:

Another simple way to get a reader interested is to tell their story by telling your story with the problem your solution solves.

The key is to switch to talking about them as soon as things get better in the story.

For example, you could write:

My teenage kids were acting out and it felt like there wasn't enough time in the day to be a good parent. Then I discovered a 40-page book which changed everything.

This book shows you how to benefit, benefit, benefit.

This is a great way to segue right into a list of bullets. Of course, more nuanced copy will describe a better life and subtly borrow clout etc. but you get the idea.

On a funny note, my father's job was to rake the visitor's area. He got paid 11 cents an hour.

What's funny about it is….as soon as he made all the parallel lines in the sand and rocks…..he would sit down and write copy which made him rich.

I also want to add to what he says about desire because he was kind of short with it.

As part of your nugget notes, describe the benefits emotionally.

You may swap "you will be able to choose what to do with your day" with "you will have the freedom to choose what to do with your day."

Describe all the benefits financially. How many hours would it take customers to learn this on your own?

How much would they spend on other books to get the same knowledge?

When you write bullets…the basic pattern should be specific/blind fact, benefit.

Only 20 Minutes leaving the rest of the day free to do anything

Why The 4 Way Guarantee Crushes The Competition

A Four Line Note Which Cuts Refunds In Half!

You will also find your second choice headlines make good bullet. tThere are no hard and fast rules; not even the rules of English apply.

There is no need to struggle making these full sentences. Abbreviate whenever possible.

I could go on and on…. but we need to keep on track.

Let's talk about action phase and making it easy for the customer to order.
Nowadays it's easier than ever to order things, but you still want to do everything you can to make the process as smooth as humanly possible.

Online shopping carts should be pre-filled out as much as possible, business reply envelopes should be pre-addressed and you should spell out what the prospect will experience when they order.

Unless you are using upselling, try to give prospects options for ordering without talking to other humans.

You should also test offering single vs. multiple ordering options.

Sometimes, only being able to order by phone boost the performance of an ad and other times multiple payment options works better. You must test.

The Boron Letters
Chapter 17

Thursday, 10:31 AM
June 28, 1984

Dear Bond,

Yesterday, the last thing I wrote about was how I want you to take the Tova "facelift ad" and copy it in your handwriting. I also said you should do this just as you would if you were going to take it to a secretarial service and have it typed.

Here's more: from now on, for the next 4 or 5 months I want you to do this same thing with other ads and DM pieces. But I don't want you to just copy any old ad or DM piece. I want you to copy only the best.

Now, here's why I want you to do all this: you see, what happens when you actually write out a good ad in your own handwriting is that the words, the flow, the sentence structure, the sequence of information, and everything else about the writing of that ad becomes a part of you.

This isn't just an empty experience. This is a way of internally imprinting on your mind and body, the process of good writing. If you do this often enough, you will soon have a deep "inside out" understanding of what it takes and what it feels like to write a good piece of copy. Now, in the beginning I want you to allow me and B. to pick which ads and DM pieces for you to copy. And, of course, the ones we will select for you to write out in your own handwriting will be those that we already know to be the cream of the crop. Ads and DM pieces that are proven winners. Ones that have brought in millions and even tons of dollars.

It is important to do this. It is one of the many disciplines that other lazy "would be" marketing geniuses will not suffer. That's too bad for them and good for us. I love that my so called "competition" is so lazy. I love it that so many people in advertising and marketing are too sophisticated, too "above" this sort of thing.

Let me tell you a little tale about a man I very much respect who was not above doing this sort of thing. He wanted to become a great writer (he was!), and so what he did was take great books and copy them (in a sense he was actually writing them) in his own hand-writing, just as I am instructing you to do. He did this for a long time. Now here is something else he took the trouble to do: since one of the books he wanted to write involved what it was like to cross the ocean under horrible conditions, what he did was travel the ocean himself in the bowels of rusty old freighters.

Well, naturally, before he was finished he had an internal deep rooted "cellular" knowledge of the process of writing a good book, and he also knew what it was like to travel the ocean in misery.

Did all of this pay off? You bet is did. This man's name is Arthur Haley and his book "<u>Roots</u>" is one of the best sellers of all time.

End of sermon. Do it. Here is a short list of "killer" promotions to get you started.

Tova Ad

**How To Burn Off
Body Fat Hour By Hour**

The Beverly Hills Diamond Ad

**The Original
Family Coat-Of-Arms
Letter**

**How To Collect
From Social Security
At Any Age**

**How To Get What
The U.S. Government
Owes You**

**The Famous Dollar Bill Letter
From The Robert Collier
Letter Book**

**The Amazing Blackjack Secret
Of A Las Vegas Mystery Man**

**The Original
Astrology Today Ad
Written By Ben Suarez**

There's more. But the above (at the rate of one per week) will keep you busy for a couple of months.

Now, here are a few other tips on how to write good copy or, as a matter of fact, "good anything." Use simple common everyday words. Use "get" instead of "procure." Write short sentences and short paragraphs. Use "transition" words and phrases to make your writing flow smoothly. Do you notice how I use transition words and phrases such as the following?

Well, as a matter of fact, I first blah...

Now, naturally, we don't want to blah, blah...

And, of course, here is what she said blah, blah, blah...

Now, here's a few more great ideas: Ask questions once in a while and then answer them yourself. Like this:

Bond, do you understand what I am saying? You do. Good, then let's go on. Etc.

How do we get the benefits? The answer is simple. All we have to do is etc., etc.

Can you imagine that? I know it seems unbelievable but facts are facts! Etc., etc., etc.

And so on. God I love to write "And so on." Kurt Vonnegut uses it quite often and he is one of the best writers I've read.

What is a good writer? Well, in my opinion a good writer is one who makes things perfectly clear. He makes it easy for the reader. Easy-to-understand what he is saying, easy to keep reading. And, if you want a treat, if you want to read an entertaining book written with great clarity, then read Vonnegut's Breakfast of Champions.

Now, don't get me wrong. I said the book was written clearly, I did not say it was written by a sane person.

Onward.

By the way, do you notice how little one word transition sentences like "onward." keep the flow going? You say you do notice? O.k., smarty, see if you can answer this question:

Question: What is the best way of becoming a good writer?

Aha! You're not absolutely certain about this one, are you?

Here is the answer:

The Best Way To Become
A Good Writer... Is By...
Writing Good Writing!

And, of course, that's what the subject of this entire letter is all about. Don't worry about developing a "style." Your own peculiarities will emerge soon enough.

But remember this. (Ran out of ink) The very best writing goes unnoticed. That's right. You don't want someone to read one of your ads and say, "Gosh, that advertisement was sure well written!"

No. What you really want is for the reader to <u>order</u> from your ad. Listen up dummy. <u>*"If you are writing for applause... you will go home with empty pockets!"*</u>

Write for <u>money</u>!

STOP
11:19

START AGAIN
6:36 PM

Here is something else to keep in mind: it is a good idea to know "word pictures" that will help your reader vicariously experience the wonderful benefits of owning your product or service. Like this:

"And, just wait untill you step into that warm, inviting jacuzzi that comes with every apartment. Man oh man! The feel of that soothing bubbling water against your bare skin is just plain heaven."

"You've heard of the expression about how you won't believe your eyes? Well, this is one time you won't believe your eyes. No kidding. The delightful aroma of these charcoal broiled steaks will remind you how good it feels to be **genuinely** *hungry"*

"Wow! When I first felt her tongue going around and around on my skin I thought I was going to scream!"

Etc. (I'm tired. These are not great examples but they'll do for now.)

STOP 6:44

START 6:46

I've got 4 minutes to go. What can I teach you in that amount of time?

Here's a little something: You can make your copy easier to read by the judicious use of parentheses. For example, if you want to tell people that your offer is good anywhere in the U.S. (except Alaska) the proper use of parentheses, as I just did, makes the copy easier-to-read, easier to understand and provides a little "eye relief" for your reader.

That's it.

STOP
6:50

I LOVE YOU
AND GOOD LUCK!

Dad

UPDATE:

I've seen a lot of people come to learn how to write copy from Gary Halbert and they are not all equal. Not everyone who followed this writing exercise became a good copywriter but everyone who did become great wrote out the winners.

This lesson should also be applied to online copy as well as sales scripts, but here is the most important update.

Kevin and I have been making videos explaining the reasoning and secrets behind our father's best work. One sharp young man started writing them out as he watches so he knows what it's like to write great effective copy, andhe also understands why most words are chosen and how it all comes together.

It's like hearing Gary Halbert's thoughts as he writes his best work.

If you want to learn more about these very popular ad breakdowns, please visit www.halbertizing.com

Also, the concept of eye-relief is more important than ever because people just don't read as much as they used to, which doesn't mean you can't write long copy.

It's just that paragraphs and sentences need to be shorter.

You know need to use a lot more ….

To Really KEEP THEIR <u>INTEREST</u>!

The key is to go through many edits..........cutting everything out until....cutting any more would be cutting something the customer would like to know.

Chop long sentences into two short ones.

Besides… short statements are more emphatic!

Break up paragraphs, and if you're writing for online, use one to two line paragraphs.

For print, try and match the style of the space you are running in.

These letters had a ton of eye-relief for the day they were written but even these letters don't have enough eye-relief for today's online standards.

The Boron Letters
Chapter 18

Friday, 7:09 AM
June 29, 1984

Dear Bond,

Well, here I am trying to get started again. Once more, I haven't the faintest idea of what I'm going to write about.

Let's see now. Oh yeah. When I left off last night, one of the last things I mentioned was how the judicious use of parenthesis (like this) can provide "eye relief" for your reader.

Alright. Now, let's talk a bit more about eye relief. Have you ever looked at a piece of writing and decided not to read it because it looked so forbidding? I'll bet you have. Many times.

Usually, this kind of writing will have long sentences, long paragraphs, narrow side margins, small type and very little white space anywhere on the page.

Now, we certainly don't want people to <u>avoid</u> reading our copy for stupid reasons like this, do we? You say you agree? Good. In that case, I'll press on.

Now, listen up. When a person first looks at something you have written it should be something that looks inviting to read. Easy-to-read. When he looks at your page of copy he should be drawn to your copy like a convict is to a Penthouse Magazine.

Your page of copy (be it letter or space ad) should be laid out in such a manner as to be an attractive "eye treat" for the reader.

This means wide margins, a certain amount of white space, double spacing between paragraphs, short words, short sentences, short paragraphs and an attractive, inviting layout.

And now, my dear son, you are about to learn one of my very most important secrets. What I am about to tell you is so important that you can get as much as 500% more readership. Yet, at the same time, this important consideration remains almost virtually unknown by almost every agency and advertising person I have ever encountered.

Listen up. Listen good and never forget what you are about to learn. Here it is:

**The Layout Of Your
Advertisement Should
Catch The Attention Of
Your Reader... But...
Not In A Way That Causes
Him To "Notice" The Layout!**

Actually, that's not as clear as it could be, is it? Perhaps I can do better. O.K., know this: In most publications, the editorial content gets 5 times as much readership as the advertising content.

Now, what does this mean on a practical basis? Simply this: It means that your ads should, as much as possible, have an "editorial look" about them.

(Better stop here and go call B. and then go to "work". Maybe I'll get to rake the sand again today!)

STOP
7:35

START AGAIN 10:37

Let's talk a bit more about the "look" of your ads and DM pieces. As I said, they should look (the ads) "editorial." However, they should not look like just any old editorial piece of writing. No. Your ads should look like an <u>exciting</u> piece of editorial material.

Here is a way to think about it: Imagine that you have written a book that you want to become a best seller. What's the best thing that could happen? Well, how about this? Suppose a guy who works as a reporter for the L.A. Times gets a copy of your book, reads it, and falls in love with it.

Now, let us further imagine that this reporter likes your book so much that he writes a full page article about our book and tells all his readers how wonderful this book is and why they should buy a copy. Wouldn't that be great? You bet!

And, just to sweeten things up even more, let us suppose that at the end of this "Rave Review" he tells his readers how to get a copy by mail. He tells them how much it costs, where to send the check or money order and who the payment should made out to!

Wow! How about that! A full page rave review that makes the reader desire the book and then tells him where and how to get it!

Now my son, listen and listen closely. Whenever you write an ad it should look, in so far as possible, exactly like a rave review written by a reporter.

It should have the look of an exciting news flash.

Here's something else. You know, whenever I want to study ad layouts, I often study editorial layouts instead.

How do we apply all this to direct mail? O.K., what would that reporter do if he wanted one of his friends in Hawaii to buy your book? The answer? Well, perhaps he would write his friend a letter and tell him the same things he told his newspaper readers.

And, perhaps he would even include a snapshot of the book so his friend would know what to look for in case he wanted to go to a bookstore to get the book. This would be one hell of a sales pitch, wouldn't it? You bet it would, and that's how your DM letters should look.

Here is a true story. Once upon a time, I wrote a letter to sell a product I dreamed up which was a family name research report. This little report would give you a short history of your family name, and it contained a black-and-white drawing of the earliest known coat-of-arms (family crest) ever to be associated with your name.

As you are aware, this became one of the most successful sales letters in history. In fact, this simple, one-page 361-word letter generated more than seven million (actually 7,156,000) cash with order customers.

Not bad, eh? But listen to what happened next! Obviously, we wanted to sell these research report buyers other products, and the logical course of action was to send them a catalog showing a bunch of products they could get that would display (in full heraldic colors!) their family crest.

Sound good to you? It sounded <u>great</u> to me. So, what I did is I went off on a camping trip by myself and there, all alone in the woods, I created a 5-1/2 x 8-1/2 four color catalog which featured about 70 attractive items that could be ordered personalized with my customer's family crest.

It bombed.

It didn't even return our mailing costs! So, what next? Well, at that point, what I did is I took the 3 best selling items in the catalog, and I put together an 8-1/2 x 11 brochure that featured only 3 items.

It did only slightly better than break even.

What?

Groan. What to do, what to do?

Here's what I did then: I wrote a very personal sales letter and I enclosed a snapshot of the best selling of the three items in the brochure. The opening of the letter went like this:

Dear Mr. Noble,

  I thought you might like to see what the Noble coat-of-arms looks like in full color so I am sending you the enclosed snapshot.

  Etc., blah, blah, blah, etc.

40 Million Dollars!

  That's right kiddo. That letter brought in 40 mil while my other "more professional" attempts fell flat on their rears.

  What's the moral here? The moral is YOU CAN DO A BETTER SELLING JOB WHEN AT FIRST IT DOES NOT APPEAR YOU ARE ATTEMPTING TO DO A SALES JOB.

  And, when I come back, the subject of my next teaching will be the importance of the fact that "YOU NEVER GET A SECOND CHANCE TO MAKE A FIRST IMPRESSION!"

                                                              STOP
                                                              11:14

                                          I love you & Good Luck!

                                                              Dad

UPDATE:

The letter he is discussing is called The Coat of Arms Letter and my dad spent 18 months revising that simple letter until he achieved what seemed like perfection.

My brother and I broke this letter down, and in my humble opinion it is the best ad breakdown in history, bar none!

In that breakdown we explain hidden psychology nobody else knew and it is loaded with hidden psychological triggers and subtle details even professional copywriters missed.

I won't do a sales pitch here, but you really should check it out over at halbertizing.com

Just look for the Coat of Arms Breakdown

Okay, back to the letter...

He is absolutely right about reducing options, which is different from packages and back-end products.

Ideally, you want to offer first-time buyers three price points.

The Cheapo Option Which Has What You Need
The Deluxe or Mid-Priced Option With Some Bells and Whistles
The Supreme Package With Prestige Service

The buyers then go to order and are offered an upsell **AFTER** they have put in their payment info.

Usually simple statements like "Others who bought this also enjoyed…IMAGE & LINK TO NEW PRODUCT.

After they have purchased, you can then sell them more products. So while my dad says to sell one thing at a time, you can make three different packages around the same key component, offer an upsell and sell many back-end products (which he will discuss later in the letters).

The Boron Letters
Chapter 19

Saturday, 9:27 AM
June 30, 1984

Dear Bond,

Today, as I promised, our subject will be "<u>You Never Get A Second Chance To Make A First Impression</u>."

Listen to this: When a person goes for a job interview, the interviewer decides whether or not to hire that person in the first <u>40-seconds</u>.

And this: In a jury trial, the members of the jury make up their minds as to whether the accused is guilty or innocent during the first half hour or so (during the opening argument), and they spend all the rest of the time the trial takes in finding ways to justify the decision they have already made.

And this: When a person falls in love, it happens almost instantaneously. After that, minor things like the truth about the newly beloved are cast aside unless those "truths" happen to reinforce the wonderfulness of said love subject.

And this: You either hook a reader or lose him when he very first looks at your ad or DM piece. Not when he reads it, but when he first <u>looks</u> at it.

Now, of course, this rule is not 100% accurate. Sometimes a person <u>will</u> suddenly fall in love with a person he or she has known for years; sometimes a jury <u>will</u> change it's mind after the opening argument; sometimes an interviewer <u>will</u> decide to hire an applicant he had originally (in his mind) rejected. And, sometimes, a reader <u>will</u> read and order from your ad, even though he was turned off by it when he first saw it.

But don't count on this. Most of the time, a person will never alter his original impression. Most of the time he will simply "edit" all new info that comes to him and "process" it in such a way as to validate his original opinion.

So, what does this mean when it comes to creating advertising? What it means is your ad or DM piece should give your prospect a life; should cause his pupils to dilate as soon as he sees it.

START AGAIN
6:10 PM

Did I ever tell you that good poker players often watch their opponent's eyes when they draw new cards? What they are looking for is to see the reaction of their opponent's eyes to the cards they draw. If their eyes widen, that is if their pupils dilate, that means that they liked the new cards they received. If their pupils constrict it probably means that what happened is that they received cards of which they are not fond.

This is a totally involuntary reaction. Apparently, what happens is that when we see something we like our eyes open up so we can let in more light and see more of it. And, conversely, when we see something we don't like we do just the opposite: we try to cut down the flow of light so we don't have to see as much of it.

Well, I have a theory about all this. What I believe is that most (or many) of our decisions about how we like or dislike something are made not in 40 seconds, or the first 4 or 40 minutes but rather in the first <u>fraction of a second</u> that we see something new.

And, I further believe that we unconsciously spend the rest of our so-called decision-making time not really making a decision after all, but instead, searching for justification for the decision we have <u>already made</u>.

And, that's why I'm so careful about the "look" of my DM pieces and MO ads. You see, I believe the "sale" or "no sale" decision is largely made the <u>instant</u> a prospect sees your ad and reads your headline.

I think that if your prospect gets an instant "lift" from just looking at your ad, then he will start reading it and <u>looking for reasons to convince himself</u> that the promise of your ad is true!

And, if you don't disappoint him, then you have a really good chance of closing the sale.

Now, what kind of look will give the reader a lift? It's short of tricky, really. But I think one thing that helps is if your promotion has a "crisp" look about it. In other words, the layout should be clean, there should be a lot of contrast, and it should look easy and inviting to read.

If you use pictures they should be, as a general rule, of an upbeat nature. Do you remember that ad with the before and after pictures of Christi Dean? You know, almost everybody liked the look of that ad because the "after" picture of Christi Dean was so uplifting.

By the way, before I forget one little-known fact that is kind of interesting, women like to see pictures of women in ads and men like to see pictures of men.

I forget why. I just remember that surveys show this to be true.

Oh, here's something else. That writer that I told you about who wrote for Printer's Ink? Anyway, his pen name was Old Aesop Glimm.

Incidentally, when it comes to direct mail, there are a number of things you can do to make your package more likely to give the reader a lift. First of all, you should use good crisp white paper, both for the pages of the letters and the envelopes you are mailing.

If you are using label addressing (and later we will discuss when you should or not), you should use a tight white label on a matching envelope.

If you are using stamps (and if you follow my advice, you almost always will) you should, whenever practical, use large colorful commemoratives.

Your letterhead should be dignified and non-distracting. Your type face should be a serif face, and you should make sure your original letter (the one you are going to use for camera ready art) should be typed with a carbon ribbon.

If you are going to use a second color in your letters to underline words or something, you should use RED. If you enclose a photograph or a simulated photograph, you should make sure it does NOT look cheap, limp and soggy. Instead, it should look crisp, clean, glossy and clear.

All those rules also apply to your enclosures.

STOP 6:53

I LOVE YOU AND
GOOD LUCK!

Dad

UPDATE:

The only thing I'd add to this is slightly higher production value than the competition applies to VSLs (video sales letters).

Everyone now uses decent sound equipment and nice cameras so it's the multi-camera and finely edited videos which stand out as professional.

Websites now have a home-made look if without using gradient color backgrounds and custom 3d buttons.

The point is going that little extra mile to add professionalism goes a long way in every aspect of marketing and the line keeps moving. Just stay one step ahead.

The Boron Letters
Chapter 20

Sunday, 12:56 PM
July 1, 1984

Dear Bond,

 A long, long time ago, Dennis Haslinger told me that most of the most serious mistakes I would make in life would be bad ego decisions.

 I have found that to be true. I have made quite a few bad ego decisions with women, many, many bad ones with money, and quite a few that put me in some sort of physical danger.

 I am trying to avoid such a mistake right now, and I am hoping that maybe writing to you about it will help. What happened, and I was playing it so loud that all that KMET rock and roll was irritating my roommates. In all truth, I was wrong in doing this and I have done it once before, and one of my roommates (the first time) had to politely ask me to turn it down.

 This time I was laying there completely lost in all this rock and roll I became aware of someone screaming my name and when I cut the radio off I could hear one of my other roommates screaming at me and telling me to show some consideration for everybody else and not to give him any "back" talk or he would break the damn thing (my radio).

 Well, how about that? It got very quiet in the room and he turned away from me and I remained silent.

 It shook me up some. Not an enormous amount but some. All kinds of things ran through my head. I wanted to explain to him that I was sorry and didn't realize I was disturbing everybody and, also I wanted to run a "macho trip" on him and tell him if he kept running his mouth I was going to rip off his head.

 And, I also thought of simply explaining to him that a better way to handle a situation like this would have been to simply tell me the volume was too loud and then I would have voluntarily turned it down.

 But I didn't do any of those things. What I did instead, as I said, is I remained silent eating a little humble pie.

Well, Bondy, I think I made a good decision. But I'll tell you, it's hard for me to live with. Unfortunately, however, that sort of thing sometimes is a part of being in prison and, in this case, the matter was a little complicated by the fact that the guy who did the yelling usually conducts himself in a way as to have very little friction with other people. He does his time quietly doing a lot of exercising and studying an accounting course.

But that - "and don't give me any back talk" really got to me, and I feel a little bit cowardly for not calling him on that. And that may have been satisfying for my ego and my pride, but it would have been really dumb.

By the way, I want to maybe surprise you a little at this point by telling you that everything in this letter has a lot to do with creating better ads and DM pieces! And don't even try to guess why at this point because I'll explain it before I am finished.

Meanwhile, back to my story: As I was saying, there was a lot of things I didn't do and I'd like to talk about why I didn't.

The first reason I didn't get tough with this guy is I was a little scared. Not much, because I am in very good shape and I am a very physical person now. But I was a little scared and with good reasons and here are some of them. First of all, this guy might have hurt me. He's pretty physical too and he has been working out in prison for years. Secondly, I might have hurt him because, as I said, I'm not exactly a guy who routinely gets sand kicked in his face. And thirdly, (and this is the big one!) if he and I had gotten in a fight we would have both been put in chains and immediately transferred to a higher security prison, PLUS we may easily have lost our "good time" and, I myself, would perhaps have had to do six months longer before I got out.

So, I think you'll agree I did the right thing but, I'll tell you, my ol' ego is having a hard time of it.

And, let's talk briefly about why I didn't explain to him a more mature way he could have handled the situation. One of the big reasons is:

I Am In Prison!

And, here doing time with me, are a lot of people who would not be here if they were capable of handling an emotionally charged situation with any kind of maturity.

So, what does all this have to do with writing sales letters and ads? It has, as I promised you, quite a lot, and here is the gist of it: Now that I've told you what I didn't do when this situation arose, I want to tell you what I did do. What I did do was stay in the room and I worked on yesterday's letter to you. And, if you will look at that letter you will see that my handwriting was somewhat shaky because of all the adrenaline working in my system.

But I did write the letter to you and then I took a walk and I went to my "thinking spot" and I plotted out my schedule for the month of July.

And this morning what I did is I did 8 long miles of roadwork on the hill. That's 10 laps. In the beginning I walked two to warm up; in the end I walked two to cool down and in the middle I jogged 6.

And what else did I do? Well, I have sat down and written this letter to you all about the event.

So, anyway, I still haven't gotten to what this has to do with writing a good sales promotion or, a "good anything" for that matter so, here it is: What I am doing, Bond, by all this writing and road work is that I am "clearing the deck" and getting (in so far as possible) this garbage out of my system so that my strategic decisions and my future letters and ideas will be clear!

Please remember this word: HALT. HALT stands for hungry, angry, lonely, and tired, and you should never make a decision when you are any of those things.

What should you do? What I did. Write, run, walk, talk, jog, etc.

But be careful who you talk with and write to. You see, it should be someone who realizes that all this must be considered as "time out babble."

You see, Bond it really doesn't matter much what the "content" of this letter is. What matters is that I am going through the "process" of writing it. And it is the process or <u>physical act</u> of the writing and the road work that does the therapy. Remember this:

You Don't Have To Get It Right...
You Just Have To Get It MOVING!

And now, in closing, let me tell you another true prison story. It is about another encounter I had that was very different than this one. You see, in the event I just described my roommate wasn't trying to "bulldog" me or shove me around. He just lost his temper in a childish way and doesn't have the "emotional tools" to respond to such a situation with maturity.

But this other one was different. You see, we have this black guy here at Boron (never mind his name) who is very strong and very loud. He lifts weights all the time and he is forever yelling (more prison talk - unprintable).

Well, as it happens, one evening I was playing pool and there weren't enough pool cues to go around. So what happens is this black guy comes into the pool room (where everybody but me is black) and starts running his mouth and while I'm racking the balls he snatches my pool cue and informs me that that is the way it was going to be.

I walked over to him and it got real quiet in that pool room. It got even quieter when I put my hands on his shoulders and my face right in front of his and said to him eyeball to eyeball:

> *"Look my friend, here's how it is. This is my stick and you ain't taking it."*

And then I took the stick away from him and resumed playing pool.

God I Hate This!

I love you and
Good Luck,

Dad

STOP 2:06

UPDATE:

When it comes to balancing ego or pride against safety… I find it best to apply one simple test which is….

What Would I Want My Son To Do?

For the most part I would like to be the ideal person my son could emulate forever.

I'd want my son to walk away from all fights he can and recognize which ones he can't which is what I do now.

I never picked on anyone but I would get so mad I'd put a hurt on people who I fully expected to give me an ass whopping.

So I don't let fear stop me but as I evolved… I truly began to envy people who have never been in a fight.

Anyway here's another important lesson…

My father taught me was to wait 72 hours after being emotional to make any important decisions.

It is hard to stay emotional for 3 days and if you still want to sue someone, leave your wife or quit your job start the process.

This little rule has saved me a ton of grief.

The Boron Letters
Chapter 21

Monday, 11:24 AM
July 2, 1984

Dear Bond,

Here I am again sitting down to write and not knowing what I am
going to write about. Yesterday was the hardest day I've had here so
far. Nothing special happened, it's just that I started really
longing for my freedom. Today my road work was so hard that I had to
divide it up into three sections and run both in the morning and
again between 10:30 and 11:30 in order to be able to finish it.

I'm tired.

Oh well, kids in Africa are starving so let's get started. I still
am stuck to let's see. Hmn? Maybe it's time we talked about
propositions. Propositions are very important. They are the "deal"
you are offering. For example: One deal might be that if you buy one
item you get another item free. Another example of a proposition is
the one used by the record and book clubs. It goes like this: *"You
can have any 10 records you want right now for only 99¢ if you agree
to buy an additional record every other month for the next two
years."* Another very common "deal" or proposition is: *"If you buy
right away you will get a big discount."* And another is: *"I'll give
you a discount if you buy more than one."* And, of course, the most

STOP
11:35

START AGAIN
4:46

common proposition of all is simply: *"If you give me X dollars I
will give you X product!"*

Propositions are very important in DM and MO selling, and a very
important ingredient in making your propositions work is the "reason
why." In other words, when you say, in effect, *"Have I got a deal
for you!"* you need an explanation as to why you are offering this
good deal.

You see, if you don't have an explanation, your "deal" won't be
believable, and you may not get the sale.

Here are some common explanations for good deals:

"I'm going out of business."

"I just had a fire and I'm having a fire sale."

"I'm crazy." (all used car dealers)

"I owe taxes and I've got to raise money fast to pay them."

"I've lost my lease and I've got to sell this merchandise right away before it gets thrown into the sheet."

"I've got to make space for some new merchandise that is arriving soon so I will sell you what I have on hand real cheap."

And so on. All of these explanations work, and that's why they are used all the time. However, there is a far more compelling "excuse for a deal," and if you can find a way to use it, you can dramatically increase your sales volume.

You know what? I just thought of something else you can do to make your copy more effective, so I am going to take a detour here and tell you about it before I forget. Don't worry. We'll come back to propositions in a minute.

Anyway, a couple paragraphs back I wrote: *"and if you can find a way to use it, you can dramatically increase your sales volume."*

Now, compare that to this: *"and if you can find a way to use it, you can make yourself a bushel of money!"*

Isn't that a lot more powerful? You bet! The words *"dramatically increase your sales volume"* do not even begin to conjure up the visual imagery of *"a bushel of money."*

So, write like that. Bring your story down to earth and hit 'em where they live. (In their hearts and their pocketbooks!)

STOP
5:05

START AGAIN
8:40

Well, Bondo, I just came up from my visit with you and Eric and it sure was good to see both of you. You know, a lot of people believe it would be better for all concerned if I never had a relationship with {name deleted} again. And they may very well be right. But I can't help it; I love her and I miss her like crazy.

And, as you probably know, Eric told me she's seeing another guy now. I can't blame her. We are broken up, and I always told her anyway that I didn't want her to wait around for me.

But boy it sure hurts.

And, once again, I'm writing about it because it releases me a little bit. You know, kiddo, you can't always control what happens to you in life, but you do have a lot of control over your responses.

So what do I do to deal with this hurt? I write. I do my road work. I do my chores. I don't snivel. And mainly:

I Just Keep On
Keepin' On

What else? I mean, unless you're going to take the pipe, there really is no other rational choice.

And so, we'll talk about that extraordinarily effective excuse for a deal. Here it is:

I Am Offering You
This Deal Because You
(By Virtue Of Some Unique Circumstance)
Are So Special

This bears a little explanation. Listen to this: Once upon a time, I wrote a letter to sell a family crest wall plaque. This letter contained a photograph of the wall plaque, just like I have talked about doing. What that letter told my reader was something like this:

> Dear Mr. So and So,
>
> I thought you would like to see what the So and So family crest looks like in full color so I am sending you the enclosed wall plaque.
>
> The reason we have the So & So wall plaque in stock is because we needed to take some pictures of our products for publicity purposes and So & So is one of the family crests we used when making our samples.
>
> However, now that we are finished with our PR campaign we have this plaque in stock with your family crest.
>
> And, since we can't sell this wall plaque to anybody unless they are named So & So we have a very limited (as you know, there aren't many So & So's) market for it.
>
> And, therefore, since your name is So & So we'd like to offer it to you at a true and honest discount of X percent!

Did this approach work? Wow! Did it ever! Like...

40 Million In Sales!

STOP
9:01

START AGAIN
9:03

You know, I'm sad, and it's hard right now to keep on keepin' on but that's what I'm going to do.

And so, as you can see, in that last example I found a way to show my customers that he was unique and valuable to me. Now, let's see if we can come up with some other ideas along this line: For example:

> "I'm offering you this special deal because your trade in is a 1976 Gas Sucker and I have a customer who wants that car. Therefore, I'm willing to break even on the sale to you make my profit from the other guy."

OR

> "Since you are one of the world's leading gynecologists, we feel you are in a unique position to appreciate this picture book of unusual_____"

OR

"Since you have proven yourself to be an astute judge of art, we are willing to send you these paintings at half price, but only if you will give us your opinion in writing."

OR

"A mutual friend of ours, Tom Smith, said I should write you because, he says, you are the best judge of value of a book like this that he knows."

Onward. Onward. Onward.

I'm hurting and the radio is playing "Amazing Grace" by, I think, Linda Ronstat. Damn! Life gets tough sometimes!

Here's more. How about this opening:

Dear Mr. So & So,

I have attached a dollar bill to the top of this letter for two reasons.

First, I needed some way to get your attention because, secondly, I have a very important message for you and every other real estate agent in L.A. County.

OR

Dear Mr. So & So,

Did you know there are only 117 So & So families in the entire U.S.?

Yes, it's true. And, because you are one of them, blah, blah, etc., etc.

STOP 9:16

I LOVE YOU AND
GOOD LUCK
Dad

UPDATE:

Surprisingly, seeing my father miss a woman never worried me because he always found someone he liked more.

Getting back to the grind…

Offering special deals based on where your promos are listed works well too.

You can offer Facebook specials and deals just for subscribers of a certain website or maybe readers of The Miami Herald.

You should also create a list of types of offers to consider and look them over when masterminding your next offer.

The Boron Letters
Chapter 22

Tuesday, 10:35 AM
July 3, 1984

Dear Bond,

O.K. Buddy, here we go again. That section on propositions and an "excuse for a deal" was quite interesting, wasn't it?

You know, I think my letters are getting a little bit random but that's O.K. I sort of think it's good to write about what pops into my mind, at least for right now, and then maybe we can review all these letters later and make something out of them that's more cohesive.

So anyway, today I'm going to start by telling you about a little trick that will improve your copywriting. And that little trick is to read your copy out loud. What happens when you read your copy out loud is that you will verbally stumble over all the places that are not smooth. Then, of course, what you do, is rewrite the rough spots and read the copy out loud again. And, what you do, is you keep repeating this process untill your copy is completely smooth and you can read it without stumbling at all.

You see, advertising writing needs to be the best writing of all. It needs to flow from start to finish without a bump or a bubble.

STOP
10:45

START AGAIN
10:46

Now, do you remember how I told you to write out in your own handwriting, good ads and DM pieces written by other people? You do remember? Good. Well, what I want to tell you here is that you should also read those same ads and DM pieces out loud. You see, by doing this writing and reading aloud of good material, you will find that the process of writing good ads will be internally

STOP
10:50

START AGAIN
11:15

imprinted on your nerves, muscle fibers, brain cells and every fiber of your being.

So, the message is clear: Get yourself a collection of good ads and DM pieces, read them aloud, and copy them in your own handwriting.

So, now what? Here I am stuck again. But not for long. What happened during my last break is I put together a deal, and I think maybe it would be a good idea at this point to talk a little about the business of mail order. Here's how some of my deals work:

What I am doing is going through the SRDS list book and looking for mailing lists that I think will yield a good profit if exploited properly.

O.K., after I have identified the list I want to go after I then start thinking about a product to sell to that list. By the way, I am especially interested in selling paper and ink and, specifically, written reports that solve a problem for the people on the mailing list. Here are some tentative titles of reports that will give you an idea of what I mean:

"How To Raise Your Child's I.Q. Before It Is Even Born!"

(for expectant mothers)

"How To Fix Your Car To Get 50% More Miles Per Gallon!"

(for owners of gas guzzlers)

"How To Collect From Social Security At Any Age!"

(I already did this one and made $800,000.00 from it.)

And so on. Well, after I have identified the list and come up with the idea for the product, I then discuss this project with one of my bankers. If he likes the project (and they nearly always do) what they do is they put up roughly about $5,000.00 to get everything going. This five thousand is used to develop the report I want to sell, to rent the test names, to pay all costs of the test, etc.

Then what happens is I create the DM promotion and have B. put it into the mail. Now then, one of three things will happen.

1.   It will be a decided loser.

   2. It will be a decided winner.

   3. It will be marginal.

 If it is a decided loser, my "banker" will have lost his $5,000.00. If it is a decided winner, my banker will then put up perhaps another $50,000 and we will mail approximately 100,000 pieces to get the ball rolling. Then, after that, we will finance the rest of the mailing from our cash flow, and my banker and I will split the profit.

 Very clean. Very neat. Very straight.

 What if it's marginal? Well, in that case, we will discuss the project again and make a judgment as to whether or not it makes sense to risk another $5,000 for another test.

 Whatever. That's the way it works and it's a nice simple way of doing business. Well, Bondy, I'm going to stop for now. I am having a pretty sad day. Don't worry though, I'm O.K., just a little heartsick.

 Such is life.

STOP
11:38

START AGAIN
2:03

 Here I am at the top of the hill in the library and once again, I'm stuck for a subject. I think a lot of it is because I have {word deleted} on my mind.

 Right now, it seems to me that I feel like outlining the steps to direct mail success so that's what I'm going to do.

   Step 1 - Find a hot market (mailing list)

   Step 2 - Find or create a product (preferably paper and ink)
            to sell to that market.

Step 3 - Create a direct mail promotion that describes the product (or service) and the benefits of owning the same.

Step 4 - Make a test mailing (1,000 to 5,000 pieces)

Step 5 - Analyze results

Step 6 - If results are good, mail 20,000 to 100,000 more letters

Step 7 - If results are still good, start rolling out and taking care of business

You know, it's really a simple procedure.

If you use good common sense, your chances of success are excellent. Where people go wrong is by making it too complicated. Actually, this is only one of the ways people go wrong, and it occurs to me that it would be helpful to enumerate the most common reasons for MO & DM failure.

And, toward this end I'm going to tell you about a little discussion I had just a couple hours ago. What happened is I was settling down writing an earlier portion of this letter when a friend of mine told me he wanted to chat with me in private. (Chat! Isn't that nifty word to describe a prison conversation?)

Anyway, what he wanted to talk about was that a friend of his had invented a gizmo that lets you make stuff out of wood the same way a key-making machine lets you make keys out of blank metal. (Actually, I don't fully understand what this thing does, but no matter.)

In any case, he wants me to take a look at the papers on this thing and see if I think it is worth promoting because the guy who invented this thing isn't following through with it because he can make so much more money smuggling dope.

Of all things! Oh my! Well, what I told him is I would be glad to help. However, I also told him that he was making the single most common mistake made by people who want to break into the MO business.

What is that mistake? The mistake is finding or developing a product FIRST and then looking for a market to sell it to. This is backasswards.

You Must Always
Find A Market <u>First</u>...

And <u>Then</u> Concentrate On A Product!

  Products are a dime a dozen. They are important, but much less
crucial to success than finding a hot market. I'll tell you this: A
guy with a new product cannot always find a hot market for that
product but a guy who has uncovered a HOT MARKET can always find a
product to fill the needs of that market.

STOP 2:22

I LOVE YOU AND
GOOD LUCK!

Dad

The Boron Letters
Chapter 23

Wednesday, 4:24 PM
July 4, 1984

Dear Bond,

Well, here I am in my room trying to avoid the heat. I heard it is 114 degrees outside right here and 120 in Palm Springs.

Whatever. We must press on. I am fasting today and I did a little bit of roadwork (just walking) a bit earlier when it wasn't so hot. I also finished doing some changes in an ad for L. and I am working on a DM letter for him. In addition, I wrote and mailed a letter to Joanie, and I am writing this letter to you.

There is a reason for telling you all this, and the reason is I want to give you some guilt.

I'm serious. I was a little disappointed during our last visit when you told me you haven't been doing your roadwork. Now, of course, if you have been sick that's one thing but, if you are goofing off just because you "feel bad" that's quite another.

Listen up, Bondy: These letters are a labor of love for me and I am trying to reach you all the important stuff I know. And, one of the most important things I can teach you is to just do it! KEEP ON KEEPING ON! Everybody else here has been eating steaks and "celebrating" the 4th. That's OK, but right now, I've got more important things to do and those are: (1) get my body in shape (2) educate my youngest son (3) make a lot of money and (4) keep up my important relationships on the outside.

And I'm doing it all. I am heartsick for my woman, I am living in 114 degree heat I have jerks for roommates, and, above all I AM IN PRISON!

And, I'm still doing it. So, you do it too. You are made out of the same stuff I am and I am so proud of you, you wouldn't believe it.

But get this. It doesn't matter how much you learn if you don't use what you learn. So when I tell you to do your roadwork and exercise with weights and study and read ads aloud and write them out in your own handwriting, I mean for you to do it and do it now!

So don't mess around with your life. I have messed up enough for both of us.

End of sermon.

Now, I'm going to talk to you about a big difference between people who make it in any field (including crime) and those who do not.

That difference is awareness.

Most people (at least many) walk around with their heads in the sand.

They are lost in a fog. They go whichever way the current of the streams of their world happens to push them. They are sheep and they are regularly shorn.

This is a bad way to be in prison. Prison is a microcosm of society and weak fish are gobbled up fast. So are those who walk around with their heads in the clouds oblivious to what is going on about them. You can't sulk in prison. You can't waste time feeling sorry for yourself. You can't stay lost in fantasies about your woman or what you are going to do when you hit the streets. No. What you must be here (and it's a good idea wherever you are!) is alert, on top of things and ready at any time to "catch a break."

Guys in prison take care of themselves. They exercise their bodies, pay attention to their grooming, read, study, and much more. You see, you never know when opportunity will knock (and it does, even here) and, if you are smart, you must be ready.

Does all this have anything to do with direct mail and mail order? You bet it does. Mail order (and all other) fortunes are made by men and women who know what's going on in their fields. These are the people who stay up to date. They read the trade journals, they make sure they are on everybody else's mailing list so they know what the competition is doing, they read all the "HOT" mail order publications, they keep their "SWIPE FILE" up to date, they read and reread the classic books written by the best people in the field, they have idea files that contain newspaper articles, notes of unusual info, hot new ideas, good layouts, unusual propositions, and so forth. They also know who the leaders are in their respective fields and they communicate with these people on a regular basis.

You know, kiddo, quite often I am referred to as an advertising genius, the "best copywriter in the world," and so forth. Now, as you know, I would be the 1st person in the world to deny these claims but if I really am so good, there is at least one reason for it that everybody misses. It is this:

I Work Like Crazy!

STOP
4:57

I just came back from the TV area and there is a guy out there who lives across the hall from me. At first, I didn't recognize him. He's a white guy, a body builder, and he has long flowing shoulder-length hair. He's been down for a long time and the reason I had a hard time recognizing him is his hair is now very short and neat. And, I'm telling you, with his short, neat hair and his no-nonsense glasses, he looks like Clark Kent. Well, anyway, I heard him explaining to another inmate that he is getting ready to go before the parole board, and he is going to make sure he doesn't give them any reason to not turn him loose.

This, my man, is the attitude to have. Always be ready to catch a break. You know, if you play enough poker, sooner or later, after thousands of hands, everybody in the game will more or less have been dealt the same amount of good hands, bad hands and mediocre hands.

What determines the winners? It's how they play the cards that were dealt them. Were they alert and ready to exploit the good ones? Did they perceive that the bad ones were in fact bad in time enough to dump them without huge losses? Were they ready to exploit or abandon their mediocre hands as the different situations dictated?

Sweat the details. It's an area I have been remiss in, and I am working to correct this state of affairs.

You do it too.

Man, am I doing a lot of writing! I've even learned to hold the pen another way when my hand gets tired from holding it the regular way~~

Oops! I lost it.

You know what? It's so hot in this room I have to keep a bandanna (it's the blue one) under my arm to keep from getting sweat stains on the paper.

And now, we're going to talk about believability. Believability is one of the top most important ingredients of good MO & DM promotions. One way to increase believability is to give exact details. Instead of "most car owners" write "77.6% of all car owners". Instead of "you can lose lots of weight" write "and the average reported weight loss over a 31-day period was 37.5 pounds for men and 26.3 pounds for women".

And, did you notice up there that when I mentioned my bandanna, I said *"it's the blue one"* in parentheses? Did you wonder why I wrote it like that? I bet you didn't. I hope not. I hope not because if you did notice, then you were noticing my writing style instead of my message.

And that's not good. However, I'll bet that little extra detail of info drew you closer to me and my letter and made this communication "more real" for you.

And, if you were a stranger, these types of details makes everything that is written that much more believable.

STOP
5:57

START AGAIN
6:00

Now, here's something else that seems to fit in my rather mish mash theme for today. It has to do with time. You know something? Most people who are on top of things and "aware" usually know what time it is within a few minutes without looking at a clock or watch.

Check yourself right now. Don't look up from this page and write down right here what time you think it is. {time you think it is _____}

Now check and see what time it actually is and write it down right here. {time it actually is _____}

How much difference is there? If there is more than 10 minutes, you are off too much. You should be able to guess with no more than a 7-minute margin of error either way.

This is one of the ways I check myself. And, if I am more than 7-minutes off, I take a walk or do something else physical before I have any important discussions or make any important decisions.

You know what got me going on about this? Of course you don't. Well, what got me going was, I looked at my watch and realized I was a full hour off!

STOP 6:09

I LOVE YOU
AND GOOD LUCK!

Dad

UPDATE:

My father's guilt worked on me with everything but roadwork. I just hate running and still do.

Every few years I pick up jogging and build up to running a few miles a day, and I just hate it.

The only marketing related update I'll add is there are many ways to add more believability, but I'm going to add a relatively new one.

Now that it's so inexpensive, video can often provide excellent proof of claims, I like to add a special twist.

In print, you can use the videos existence as proof by saying, "our customers have taken to YouTube to share their success stories."

I like to offer video testimonials whenever possible, and I will write out the main thing I want them to hear in a quote directly below the video like so.

****

VIDEO

****

"… Bond's advice doubled my profits!"

This way, readers don't even have to look at the video to get the main point, and the fact that the video is there adds more believability than static testimonials.

As I said, there are lots of ways to add believability to your offers. You can read more of my dad's advice over at halbertizing.com

The Boron Letters
Chapter 24

Thursday, 7:15 AM
July 5, 1984

Dear Son,

 Well, I'm feeling better today. I think these short, frequent days of fasting are really cleaning me out. I really feel a need now, more than ever, to shed my excess weight because it is starting to get really hot here. In fact, I'll bet it's 80 degrees or so already this morning.

 Anyhow. What I want to tell you this morning is that after tomorrow I am going to stop writing these letters for a while. There are several reasons: For example, I need to review some reference material and take notes and then, more or less outline, the future letters as my babblings seem to me to be getting too random. Another thing is that I want you to get this first batch of 25 letters typed up so I can easily review them and take notes from them also. And, also, I need to catch up on some of my other work like filing my rule 35 motion (a request for a modification of sentence) so I'll have a chance of getting out of here earlier.

 And, finally, I have a couple of "bankers" who are eager for me to develop some promotions which they will finance and then we will split any profits 50/50.

 And you know what? I think an excellent way for you to learn how to make money in this business is to watch over my shoulder as I begin to create one profitable promotion after another.

 Here's how I'm going to start: First of all, I am going to go through the SRDS book and make a note of all the lists that look like hot markets. Then, I'm going to show Eric this list of lists and ask for his comments. I'm sure he will be able to add to my lists and maybe he will also be able to tell me that some of the lists are really not so hot.

 In any case, after all that, I will have a page full of list selections and I will write you a letter telling you what lists I have selected. After that, I will put on my thinking cap and develop some product ideas to try and sell to the various lists. By the way, I would very much appreciate any ideas that pop into your head after you see my list of lists. Well, in any case, after all this, I will sleep on it and then, pretty soon, I will codify (isn't that a neat word) and isolate the projects I want to work on.

Then I'll talk to my bankers.

Here's the way it works with my bankers. If they see a project they would like to be involved with, they will have to come up with a development fee of $5,000.00. (Believe me, that's peanuts to these guys.) This $5,000.00 will be used to create a DM piece and to make a test mailing of that piece to 2-5M names. We will also use some of the money for product development.

O.K. after that, if the response is no good, the banker will eat his $5,000.00 loss and we will go on to the next project.

If, however, the results look good, we will then proceed to a larger mailing of perhaps 50,000 pieces. And then, after we get our results from the 50,000 pieces, if everything still looks good, we will start rolling out and taking care of business.

It's a good outline, I think. I intend to keep you informed every step of the way, and I'll let you "live" the development of these projects with me. And, as a matter of fact, I think I will let you help me with some of these projects and give you a small cut of the action.

So, sharpen your driving skills. Do your roadwork, and get cracking on all those other things I told you were good things to do. I'll join you again on my lunch hour.

STOP
7:40

START AGAIN
3:12

Well, kiddo, it's past the lunch hour, but better late than never, eh? Whatever. I'm stuck for a theme again. What do you suggest? O.K. How about the subject of IMPACT? Good, I'm glad you agree.

Impact is the impression you or your promotion makes on its intended target. Someone once said that the average American is subjected to about 1,500 commercial messages every day. Probably so. Especially when you count billboards, ads on TV, ads on radio, ads on the backs of buses, on taxicabs, on match covers, in newspapers, magazines, direct mail pieces, etc., etc.

However, out of all those ads very very few have any appreciable impact. And impact is one of the things I strive for.

STOP

START AGAIN
9:17

And, what I want to talk about right now is my favorite way in all the world to achieve impact with my DM promotions. What I'm talking about is attaching things to the top of my letters. I've mentioned this before, but now I want to go into it in considerably more detail.

The best letter <u>ever</u> to use this technique was the classic "dollar bill" letter featured in "The Robert Collier Letter Book." (must reread)

This was a first class letter that was designed to raise funds for a children's hospital. When the recipient opened the envelope, he discovered a personal, typed letter with a real, honest-to-goodness dollar bill attached to it. The copy explained that the writer wanted to donate a thousand dollars to a certain children's hospital, but that he realized that a thousand dollars wouldn't go very far. So, what he (the writer) had decided to do was divide his $1,000.00 contribution into 1,000 - one dollar bills and then mail these bills to 1,000 different people. Now, he went on to say, what he hoped is that everybody who received one of these dollar bills would decide not to keep it and, instead, send it straight to the hospital with one or more dollars of their own.

Did it work? Oh my! It was probably the most effective direct mail promotion ever mailed. It got better than a 90% response, and the people to whom it was mailed eventually contributed tens of millions of dollars!

That's Impact!

Today, in the mail, I received a copy of my Japanese "Penny" promotion. This promotion, as you know, has a Japanese "Penny" attached to the top of the letter, and the copy says that the writer is attaching the penny to the letter for two important reasons.

The first reason is to get attention. And, secondly, because what the letter has to talk about was discovered in Japan, the writer felt that some sort of "Japanese" eyecatcher was appropriate.

This letter is working like crazy. It has impact.

But, be careful. Whatever you attach to the top of your letters should tie in with the rest of your letter and what you are selling. It should make sense and fit into the promotion in a natural way.

Here is an example of how not to use impact: Some companies print up advertising that, at first glance, looks like a traffic ticket. Then, they hire kids to put these traffic ticket-type ads on the windshields of parked cars.

What happens is, that the owner of the car comes back to discover what seems to be a traffic ticket on his windshield and he, naturally, grabs it forthwith and starts to read it.

It sure gets his attention. It sure achieves impact. The guy will sure remember that company.

**But He Will Remember The
Company With Distaste!
He Will Remember That This
Is A Company That Scared
Him And Made Him Angry!**

You know what all that adds up to?

No Sale!

STOP
9:40

START AGAIN
9:42

The message is clear: You must not use "cheap tricks." Make what you attach to the letter "fit in." All it takes is a little imagination. Let's see if I can come up with a couple of original examples:

How about attaching an eagle feather to a letter that tells how these birds are in danger of becoming extinct?

How about attaching a Mexican Peso to a letter that talks about inflation? I did it and it was a great puller.

How about a computer microchip attached to a letter that explains why a certain new electronic product is superior to the competition?

How about my son attaching a picture of himself to a letter to his old man that tells him how he is getting into good shape?

How about you send me some ideas along these lines?

STOP 9:48

I LOVE YOU
AND GOOD LUCK!

In this letter, my father mentions bankers. It's every creative marketer's dream to have a capable and energetic partner who handles all the logistics of managing the business but it rarely works out.,

Here is the natural evolution of a copywriter.

After studying the art of copy, most newbies struggle a lot to land jobs.

They have a few failures, and eventually write a winning ad for a client or two.

Soon, the word of his success gets around, and all of a sudden others want to talk about hiring the new hot shot.

The writer soon learns it takes a lot these to research and write effective sales copy for a particular market, so copywriters naturally begin to get more hits in one field and begin to specialize.

Not wanting to deal with all the hassles of finding new clients and selling them on how great their copy is, the writer soon finds life easier working for just one or two clients.

These are the clients they write winning ads for, and these business owners begin to dominate the copywriter's workload.

Then one of two things happens.

Either...

    A) An ad or two fails to produce profits

or

B) The client refuses to keep handing over money for what they consider to be a few hours of work done a long time ago

No matter which case happens, the writer soon finds themselves in a bad situation.

They have been off the market and now they struggle to find work.

By this time, they usually partner with an old friend who wants to tap into their success or start their own business (usually selling a copywriting course).

This isn't every copywriter's tale, but it's close enough to illustrate how and why the top ad men like to work with a few professional clients and/or starting their own businesses.

The best copywriters love to write and keep taking clients, but to get them, you need something profitable, easy, and very interesting to snag them away from other opportunities.

In this letter my father mentions using a dollar bill as a great grabber (and it is), but I will tell you about a better one in just a moment.

First I want to make the point that in a pinch, a dollar will work as a great grabber for almost any product with a margin of profit high enough to be worth adding a whole dollar to the cost per lead.

You can say the reason this seemed appropriate is it relates to saving money, making money, or as the first dollar they can put towards buying your product.

But, if you are planning on mailing a list at least twice, thanks to my dad, I think I have found a better way.

You see, among my father's things, I found a stack of Iraqi dinars and knew instantly he thought they would be good grabbers, yet I had no product to use them for until a few years later.

Allow me to get side-tracked for a moment…

I like to experience human energy in mass so…. if there is a huge crowd, I like to meander about by myself.

Every Christmas season, I finish all my shopping early enough to go casually walk around the crowded malls.

I check out almost any large protest, and on one such occasion I had a brainstorm at a political rally.

It was an early Tea Party rally, and I saw how fired up they were. It inspired me to come home and type up a sales letter using the dinar.
Here is the beginning…

Dear Mr. Everett,

As you can see, I have attached a crisp Iraqi Dinar to the top of this letter.

I did this for two reasons.

1) I needed some way to get your attention and since what I have to say concerns the falling US dollar, it seemed especially appropriate.

2) This Iraqi Dinar is going to help me prove what I have to say.

You see this currency is basically worth less than the paper it is printed on, because even blank paper has some value.

However, some savvy people _made millions_ of US dollars from the fall of the Iraqi Dinar, and in a moment, you will know…

**Exactly How They Made So Much Money
From The Fall of This Doomed Currency!**

And, how you can benefit from the same knowledge.

You see, what made this Dinar so worthless was the _decisions_ made by the man whose face is on the front of it.

And…

If you sense the decisions being made right now by _our own government_ are _hurting_ the American Dollar, this may be <u>the</u> <u>most</u> <u>important</u> <u>message</u> <u>you</u> <u>will</u> <u>ever</u> <u>read</u>!

Here is why…

1. When the government started spending **billions** and **billions** of dollars bailing out Wall Street fat cats and banks, I knew this was not good news for the good ole US Dollar, and I was right.

As our government fired up the printing press, it made me mad, and then it just bummed me out. Eventually, I even began to panic and started to wonder if it would become difficult to feed my family until…

I heard about a guy who taught me, and he can show you…

**How To Use The Situation
To Make Life Better
For You and Your Family!**

I haven't worried since and when you are finished reading this, you will realize there is a way out of the danger, and you will worry a whole lot less too.

There are a growing number of Americans waking up to the reality that the US dollar is going down the tubes. They are getting nervous, and they even refer to the complete collapse of the US dollar as…

"The Impending Event!"

Many of these good Americans have the right idea, but they are ignoring the…

**Single Best Way To Prepare For
The Collapse Of The US Dollar!**

Don't make the same mistakes they are by relying only on emergency food rations, ammo, and gold.

Then the letter would use lot of conservative language which would explain how some good Americans are preparing for the future but going about it the wrong way.

I explain how investing in gold won't cut it and that there is a better way.

I talk about how passing spending bills lowers the value of the dollar which means places like Switzerland can't sell us as many Rolex watches so they pass their own massive spending bills to devalue their own money and keep jobs.

As this goes on throughout the world, the news of such spending bills will drive wild swings in the FOREX or foreign exchange markets and here is a FOREX system they can buy.

Now I like this better using the Dinar better than the dollar bill for several reasons:

1. The reader can't spend it so it can sit around reminding them
2. It's cheaper than a $1
3. It is more memorable.

This last point is where the real power is.

Believe it or not ,some people have received more than one dollar bill letter, and you can make serious hay out of your follow up mailing if your grabber is this memorable.

Dear Mr. Everett,

As you can see, I have attached this fake million dollar bill and I did so to make a point.

You may recall from my last letter with the Iraqi Dinar attached that I talked about the fluctuations in the dollar and investing in gold.

Well I'm proud to say that depending on the timing, if you had invested in gold, depending upon the timing you could have earned 10%or potentially lost 30% but….

Since I last wrote to you, the fluctuations in the foreign exchange market have netted investors a return of 300%!
Blah blah blah

The reason I like this better is a Dinar can't be spent or given to the kids and since it is theoretically money, few people throw it away. This means it sits around a lot reminding them of my Forex offer.

Now when I remind the reader about the previous letter they think "oh yeah, I remember that. In fact, I think it's still around here."

Now it is rare, but some people do see more than one dollar bill letter, but who else would have sent them an Iraqi Dinar?

The ability to remind them of you previous message is priceless because the prospects feel they got to know you a little over two letters, and it allows you to make an effective "I told you so" argument to say "gold has done so but had you listened to me you would be sitting pretty."

Friday, 7:14 PM
July 7, 1984

Dear Bond,

Tonight I am going to be writing about something I didn't think I was going to be writing about.

I just had a minor confrontation in the chow hall with a guy I've had a little trouble with before. He was giving out cups of ice and when I insisted on two cups, he said, "no" and we verbally got into it. At one point, he suggested that if I didn't like his refusal to give me more ice, we could go fight behind one of the dorms.

I glared at him and walked away. We were starting to attract attention and there were (always are) guards in the mess hall.

Really, this is no big deal except in a way, it is. This guy is not very much like the roommate I had some trouble with. This guy is young, tattooed and stupid. He is a loser and I know from previous conversations with him that he is pretty much lost when he is on the street.

He is always messing up, he smokes dope, and he is in the Lieutenant's office often for disciplinary action.

I would probably kick the living **** out of this guy. You never know for sure, I could be wrong but he is not a big, bad type. Mostly, he is just plain stupid.

But what may be instructive in all this is why it happened and what I hope to do about it so I, hopefully, don't have to deal with it again.

First of all, let me explain that both the incident with my roommate and this incident happened when I was "off". As a matter of fact, I am off right now and I have been off for more than a week. When I am off, when anybody is off, this is communicated!

Right now, also, (or in conjunction with) being off, I am also quite vulnerable. I have fasted two days this week, I am missing L. and I have been, in general, feeling sad.

No big deal. Except when you are in prison. When you are in prison, even a very easy one like this one, your "Karma", I believe, is extra important! It's important on the street too, but it is especially important here. This is a bad place to be weak, even a little and even momentarily.

Remember how I told you, you could sort of tell if you were off by how close you could guess what time it is? Well, another indicator is if you bump into things just a tiny bit or you are just a tiny bit clumsy. Don't forget HALT. Hungry. Angry. Lonely. Tired. When I went into that mess hall, I was all of this except angry and I was probably a little angry too.

Now, here's an interesting thing about both of these two incidents. In both cases, I was "wrong." Not big deal wrong. But wrong from a not-being-aware-and-on-top-of-things aspect. You see, in the incident with my roommate, if I had been aware, I would have realized that my radio was causing an infuriating disturbance. And, in this recent incident in the mess hall, I should have realized that this guy was deliberately positioned there for the *express purpose of rationing out the ice, and here I was responding to his "What about the rest of the guys?"* with the answer, *"To hell with the rest of the guys!"*

And, believe it or not, I said that a little unconsciously because I sort of thought he was joking. You see, I just wasn't on top of things.

On the street, neither of these things would have been a big deal. But here, there is a <u>lot less</u> slack.

So, now that I know I'm off, what do I do? Well, I certainly don't intend to fight this guy who I refer to as "The Rodent." That could cost me six months extra in the joint. But, I don't want many more of these incidents either. So, what I intend to do is lay low for a while until I am feeling strong and not feeling vulnerable.

You know why I'm going to lay low? It's because I'm concerned. Not physically scared ("The Rodent" isn't very threatening) but concerned that I better get back on top mentally to be more prepared to deal with this environment.

Does it seem like I'm making a big deal out of all this? Don't kid yourself. It's serious. I'm missing L like crazy right now, I am missing my freedom, I am angry about having to be here, I am diminished by my previous confrontation, I am weak from fasting, I am tired (albeit pleasantly) from my long run and all the time I spend in the sun and, in general, I am a bit weakened.

I am starting to make mistakes.

No good. Not here. So, what I intend to do is fall back and regroup.

                                                  STOP
                                                  7:46

START AGAIN
7:48

I am, for a little while, going to try to avoid (as far as possible) my fellow inmates. I'm going to fast tomorrow and sort of hide out. I don't intend to fast again after that for another week. You know, when I'm on the street (God, I even talk like a con now!) I also avoid people whenever I fast and it is even more important here.

So, first I'm going to lay low and secondly, I am going to try not to "emerge" until I have pumped a little iron.

You know, I may be wrong but, I think had I been "pumped" neither of these incidents would have happened. I think this for two reasons:

1)   I would have been more alert and never did the things that perpetuated these incidents.

    2) And secondly, when I am "pumped" and on top of things, people react differently to me because I send out different "vibes."

By the way, another way I can tell I am stressed right now is my vision is a little blurred.

So now, after all this preamble can I relate any of this to your success at DM and MO? You bet. At the time in my life when I was making the most money, I followed the same procedure I am talking about here. Namely: I pay attention to myself and when I am off, I drop out of sight and do what is necessary to strengthen myself.

It is important here, it is important out there, and it is especially important in business dealings. People can smell it when you are weak. When you are vulnerable. They can smell success too.

They can sniff out a winner.

And you can't fake it. Not for long. You've got to _be_ it!

                                                  STOP
                                                  7:59

START AGAIN
8:03

Lord I'm tired. My vision is more blurred. And, I have just made some minor but maybe important changes in my planned routine over the next little piece of time. I'll tell you what they are when I resume writing.

                                                          STOP
                                                          8:05

START AGAIN 9:31

What I have decided is, I had better not take a day off running right now. I intend to run in the morning and fast tomorrow. And, then, run again Sunday, even though I fasted the day before. What I'll do I think, is I'll get up early like (sun up) 5AM and eat a couple oranges and drink a little coffee and maybe take warm up shower or a longer than normal warm up walk and then run Sunday too.

Boy, did I just have a good talk! I found a guy here who is very much like me. His life is stones, he's intelligent, he's Cherokee Indian and he has had some "incidents" also and he gave me some good advice.

He said you can't sink to their level. Just don't talk to them. He also said avoid cursing. And, it's funny; he does the same stuff I do: He runs, he pumps iron, etc. Maybe a valuable friend.

I'm so tired. I really want to get out of here now.

Since this is the last of my first batch of letters (this is #25) to you, I am going to try and think of something extra, maybe a little special to say.

I don't know what. Let's see. How about this? One of the things I have learned here is how precious the good times and the good people are. I hope I have learned never again to not take care of my special relationships.

Like the one I have with you. Let's remember we've got something very special and really take care of it.

                                                   I LOVE YOU AND
                                                   GOOD LUCK!

                                                      Dad

                                            Type up a sales9:42

START AGAIN 9:44

P.S.   I've got four more minutes to do to get my hour in. Let's see.
   I guess what I want to focus on here at the end is my resolve to
   "go underground" and quietly strengthen myself. I've really got
   to do it. I've got to transcend myself.

   And, what I think my theme will be is to make a game of
   becoming an expert at quietly diffusing explosive situations and
   sending out stronger vibes so I have fewer (or maybe none)
   encounters to begin with.

That's It!

STOP
9:48

This last letter is great.

Being off happens to all of us, and it is super important to know when you are off.

Besides the tricks my dad talks about, I also found you can use Sudoku puzzles to gauge how off you and even better...

You Can Use This To Warm Up Your Brain

The brain is like any other human muscle. It needs proper nourishment and rest and can be exercised to work better.

When I am off, I struggle to finish the diabolical level Sudoku puzzles, but when I'm on fire, I can rip through them really fast.

Since they are 100% logic-based, they are better than crosswords and other brain teasers because one is not much trickier than another and no special knowledge is being measured.

You may not like Sudoku puzzles, but try and find a good way to determine when you are sharp and try and find something you can do to warm up the ole noodle.

Being on or off makes a HUGE DIFFERENCE in your success.

Ever have a problem that seemed insurmountable, and after calm reflection you realize you can handle everything with one easy step? Everyone has.

When you are on fire, rock and roll. Just keep pumping out copy, cutting deals and make the most out of that energy.

But, when you are down, do as Pop suggests and work while you hide out.

Life really is like high school, and despite what people say, nobody wants to help or be with the sulking kid.

By doing work alone, you will not only avoid allowing others to smell your weakness, but you will cause an air of mystery.

The cool kids are always of doing something nobody else knows about.

By working independently, even if angry, you will come out on a more solid footing which will be evident in your attitude.

The last point I'm going to make is about taking care of your good relations.

When I'm down there is nobody I like to be around more than my wife. She is super supportive and a perfect example of the kind of relationship worth investing in, but all that aside, the lesson which needs to be added is...

Drop The Dead Weight!

My relationship with my father and mother has always been really strong, but one thing I learned from both of them is not to waste time with people who are simply dead weight.

Unless the Hindus are right, we all get only one go-round in life, and time is too precious to waste on people who undermine your confidence, hold petty grievances and don't add to your enjoyment of life.

My dad was a very loyal chap who would stand by all his good friends, but he would cut his own mother out of his life if she didn't add more than she took away.

Your respect for others means a lot more when you have enough self-esteem to never respect those who don't respect you.

You can learn to respect yourself by creating your own moral code and standing by it.

Well I hope you have enjoyed these letters as much as I have. For more great newsletters and marketing wisdom you really should check out Halbertizing.com

Made in the USA
Middletown, DE
17 January 2020